INVESTIGATIONS IN ENVIRONMENTAL SCIENCE

Unit 1: Land Use

A CASE-BASED APPROACH TO THE STUDY OF ENVIRONMENTAL SYSTEMS

Daniel C. Edelson Ph.D.

Developed by

The Geographic Data in Education (GEODE) Initiative

Northwestern University

GEODE INITIATIVE

Geographic Data in Education

In association with

IT's ABOUT TIME®

HERFF JONES EDUCATION DIVISION

HERFF JONES EDUCATION DIVISION
84 Business Park Drive, Armonk, NY 10504 Phone (914) 273-2233
Fax (914) 273-2227 Toll Free (888) 698-TIME (8463) www.its-about-time.com

It's About Time, President
Tom Laster

Director of Product Development
Barbara Zahm, Ph.D.

Creative/Art Director
John Nordland

All student activities in this textbook have been designed to be as safe as possible, and have been reviewed by professionals specifically for that purpose. As well, appropriate warnings concerning potential safety hazards are included where applicable to particular activities. However, responsibility for safety remains with the student, the classroom teacher, the school principals, and the school board.

Printed and bound in the United States of America.

ISBN 978-1-58591-444-9

2 3 4 5 6 VH 11 10 09 08 07

This material is based upon work supported by the National Science Foundation under grants No. RED-9453715, ESI-9720687, DGE-9714534. Any opinions, findings, and conclusions or recommendations expressed in this material are those of the author(s) and do not necessarily reflect the views of the National Science Foundation.

Project Director
Daniel C. Edelson Ph.D.

Lead Curriculum Developers
Kathleen Schwille
Meridith Bruozas
Michael Lach
Michael Taber
Douglas Gordin

Curriculum Developers
Kylene Chinsio
Natalie Goldstein
Adam Tarnoff

Lead Developer, Teacher Edition
Ann Rivet

Developer, Teacher Edition
Amy Emmert

Consultants
Duane Griffin
Brad Sageman

Contributors
Janet Bell-Wehr
Jennifer Coyle
Matthew Cruz
Douglas Goodwin
Lisa Kenyon
Shanna McGarry
Petra Pancoskova
Cynthia Quinn
Colleen Riley
Marc Siciliano
Darlene Slusher
Craig Smith
Susan Trzaskus

Pilot And Field Test Teachers
Janet Bell-Wehr
Lori Blackburn
Anne Bogardt
Staci Bynum
Patricia Carlson
Mollie David
Julie Dowling
Theresa Dzoga-Borg
Jayne Entihar
Roger Felch
Linda Fleming
Douglas Goodwin
Nina Hike-Teague
Lloyd Kiefer
Gloria Latta
Cynthia Lauster
Chris Nichols
Phyllis Nicholson
Lars Nelson
Danielle Oplaski
John Pritchard
Gwynna Reinhardt
Delvena Riggins-Dawes
Antoinette Rubalcaba
Cliff Schlund
Tamara Shibayama
Marc Siciliano
Julia Somers
Dawn Teaschner
Peter Thomas
Susan Trzaskus
Ray Tschillard
Eric Wheeler
Steve Wilson

Programmers
Brian Clark
Peter Moore
Eric Russell
Christopher Kadel
Ben Loh
Laura Ferguson
Hisham Petry

Geospatial Data Development
Terry Hammarquist
Michael Smith

Undergraduate Research Assistants
Eddy Ameen
Tajuana Bates
Eric Hanson
Aaron Hosmon
Benjamin Johnson
Steve Juh
Danielle Lessovitz
Ray Liu
Michael Nam
Viktoria Wang

Evaluation
SRI International
Principal Investigators:
Roy Pea
William Penuel
Dan Zalles
Valerie Crawford
Yukie Toyama

The Learning Partnership
Principal Investigator:
Steven McGee

WorldWatcher Curriculum Project
Daniel C. Edelson,
Principal Investigator
Louis M. Gomez,
Co-Principal Investigator

Advisory Board

James Hays, Ph.D.
Lamont-Doherty Earth Observatory
Columbia University

James Hansen, Ph.D.
NASA Goddard Institute for Space Science

George Tselioudis, Ph.D.
NASA Goddard Institute for Space Science

Mary Marlino, Ph.D.
Digital Library for Earth Systems Education,
University Corporation for Atmospheric Research
Boulder, CO

Kathryn Keranen
Great Falls, VA

Mary Ellen Verona, Ph.D.
Maryland Virtual High School
Silver Spring, MD

Mark Horrell, Ph.D.
Illinois Math and Science Academy

Prassede Calabi, Ph.D.
Black Cat Consulting
Winchester, MA

Herbert Their
Lawrence Hall of Science
University of California, Berkeley

Joe McInerney, Ph.D.
National Coalition for Health Professional Education in Genetics

Michael Goodchild, Ph.D.
National Center for Geographic Information and Analysis
University of California, Santa Barbara

External Reviewers

Derek Aday, Ph.D.
Department of Evolution, Ecology, and Organismal Biology
Ohio State University

Heidi Anderson
Yellowstone Center for Resources

Comfort Ateh, Ph.D.
University of California, Davis

Denis Bacon, Ed.D.
College of Agricultural Sciences and Technology
California State University, Fresno

Dave Bayless, Ph.D., P.E.
State of Ohio Coal Research Center
Ohio University

Jason Box, Ph.D.
Department of Geography
Ohio State University

Carrie Schaefer Bucki

Michael Cain
Department of Applied Biology
Rose-Hulman Institute of Technology

Will Cantrell, Ph.D.
Physics Department
Michigan Technological University

Susan Cassels
Office of Population Research
Princeton University

Michael Chang, Ph.D.
School of Earth & Atmospheric Sciences
Georgia Institute of Technology

Ian Clark
School of Natural & Built Environment
University of South Australia

Barbara Cooper, Ph.D.
Purdue University

John Costa
U.S. Geological Survey

David Flaspohler, Ph.D.
School of Forest Resources & Environmental Science
Michigan Technological University

Rong Fu, Ph.D.
School of Earth & Atmospheric Sciences
Georgia Institute of Technology

Brett Hamlin, Ph.D.
School of Engineering
Michigan Technological University

Jerry Hatfield
USDA/ARS National Soil Tilth Laboratory

L. Gregory Huey, Ph.D.
School of Earth & Atmospheric Sciences
Georgia Institute of Technology

Craig Kallsen
Farm Advisor
University of California, Cooperative Extension

Mary Kleb
NASA Langley Research Center

Brian Kloeppel, Ph.D.
COWEETA Hydrologic Laboratory
University of Georgia

John LaBoon
U.S. Bureau of Reclamation

Nathanael T. Lauster, Ph,D.
University of British Columbia

Kevin Lien
Portland Community College

Joseph Moran, Ph.D.
American Meteorological Society
University of Wisconsin, Green Bay

John Mull, Ph,D.
Department of Zoology
Weber State University

Larry Nuss
U.S. Bureau of Reclamation

Rebecca Redhorse, M.S.

William Reinert, Ph.D.

Ron Reuter, Ph.D.
Department of Forest Resources
Oregon State University, Cascades Campus

Jennifer Rhode, Ph.D.
Department of Biology and Environmental Science
Georgia College and State University

George Rudins
U.S. Department of Energy

Del Smith, P.E.
U.S. Bureau of Reclamation

Michelle Sneed
California Water Science Center
U.S. Geological Survey

John Richard Stepp, Ph.D.
University of Florida

Lynn Wright
Oak Ridge National Laboratory

Don Wuebbles, Ph.D.
Department of Atmospheric Sciences
University of Illinois

Safety Reviewer

Carl Heltzel
Transylvania University

Unit One Photography Credits

COVER PHOTOS: Getty Images, Robert J. Williams

Chapter 2: Populations

LESSON 1 DAPHNIA (PAGE 12): Photo of Daphnia courtesy Luc Ducazu, www.daphnia.com;

LESSON 2 BASIC ARCVIEW SKILLS, ADVANCED ARCVIEW SKILLS, MORE ARCVIEW PRACTICE, ARCVIEW TIP SHEET (PAGES 21-32): All ArcView screenshots courtesy ESRI;

LESSON 3 POPULATION DEPTH (PAGE 35): World population data courtesy U.S. Census Bureau, International Data Base;

LESSON 3 POPULATION PYRAMIDS (PAGES 39-42): Population pyramids courtesy U.S. Census Bureau, International Data Base;

LESSON 3 BIRTH RATE AND DEATH RATE (PAGE 47): Canadian birth and death rate information adapted from The Statistics Canada website, http://www.statcan.ca/english/Pgdb/popula.htm, June 2004.

(*Statistics Canada information is used with the permission of Statistics Canada. Users are forbidden to copy this material and/or redisseminate the data, in an original or modified form, for commercial purposes, without the expressed permission of Statistics Canada. Information on the availability of the wide range of data from Statistic Canada can be obtained from Statistic Canada's Regional Offices, Its site at http://www.statcan.ca, toll-free access number 1-800-263-1136);*

LESSON 4 REINDEER ON ST. MATTHEW ISLAND (PAGE 50): Reindeer photograph taken by Mathew Magimai Doss in Ranua Zoo, Lapland, Finland (Dec. 2001);

LESSON 4 REINDEER ON ST. MATTHEW ISLAND (PAGE 51): Reindeer population data courtesy David R. Klein, Professor Emeritus, Institute of Arctic Biology, University of Alaska, Fairbanks.

Chapter 3: Resources

LESSON 1 SUSTAINABILITY AND ECOLOGICAL FOOTPRINTS (PAGE 74): Ecological footprint data courtesy Redefining Progress;

LESSON 2 MEETING THE DEMAND FOR ENERGY (PAGE 94): Energy consumption graphs courtesy Energy Information Administration;

Chapter 4: Ecosystems

LESSON 1 GOPHER TORTOISES (PAGE 142): Photo of gopher tortoise courtesy Michael J. Connor, Ph.D.;

LESSON 2 FOOD CHAINS (PAGE 150): Pine Flatwoods image courtesy Florida Panther Net;

LESSON 2 BIOMAGNIFICATION (PAGE 156): DDT Biomagnification image courtesy John W. Kimball.

Dear Student,

Welcome to *Investigations in Environmental Science*. Your experience in this course may be different from the courses you have taken before. We designed it that way to help you develop a different kind of science understanding.

The most important difference is that *Investigations in Environmental Science* places you in the position of an environmental scientist. This course will present you with challenges to work on that are just like the ones that real environmental scientists work on. Of course, we know that you are a student, not a scientist. So, this course will help you develop the knowledge and skills you need to work on the challenges.

Each unit in *Investigations in Environmental Science* will present you with an environmental challenge. It will then help you to learn the science you need to work on that challenge. Each unit ends with a project where you will use the science you have learned to propose a solution to the unit's challenge. The stories behind each challenge are fictional. However, they are based on real problems faced by real communities. We use these stories to help you understand how science is used in the real world and to help bring the challenges to life for you.

To help you select a solution to each challenge, you will learn a process for making decisions about environmental issues. This process asks you to consider all the effects of a decision including the costs and benefits for both humans and the environment. This decision-making process allows people with different values to come to different decisions. However, before they apply their values, they must use their understanding of science to identify the effects of their decisions. In this way, you will learn how science can be used to predict the effects of our actions, and how those predictions can be used to reach decisions.

A second difference from most other science courses is that in *Investigations in Environmental Science* you will use computer software extensively. In this course, you will learn how to use a computer program called a geographic information system or "GIS." Environmental scientists use GIS software to map and analyze data about the environment. You will use GIS software to help you understand your environmental challenges. We believe that it is important for students to learn to use the same computer tools scientists use because that will help you understand how today's scientists work.

The final important difference between *Investigations in Environmental Science* and other textbooks is how it is organized. *Investigations in Environmental Science* is not organized by topic. *Investigations in Environmental Science* is organized around the problems you will be working on. You will learn about a topic when it will help you to make progress on a problem.

In this course, you will learn the same content you would learn in a traditional environmental science course. However, in this course you will learn it as you work on specific environmental problems. We decided to organize *Investigations in Environmental Science* this way because research shows that people learn things better when they have a reason to learn it. We have selected the problems you will work on in this course to give you a good reason to learn the science.

It is very important for people in modern society to understand environmental science. We have created *Investigations in Environmental Science* to help students across the country understand the complex relationships between humans, the other living things on Earth, and the environment we share. However, we know there is only so much that you can learn in one course. We hope that this course will encourage you to learn more about environmental science and to share your knowledge with others throughout your lifetime.

Sincerely yours,

Daniel C. Edelson
Editor, *Investigations in Environmental Science*

TABLE OF CONTENTS

New School

Chapter 1
New School

Connections

School overcrowding is a common problem in many communities. In your own school, you may have portable classrooms, shared lockers, and limited parking space. In this chapter and unit, you will explore the problem of school overcrowding and think about possible solutions.

You will look at issues that cause school overcrowding. The main issues are an increasing number of students and a limited amount of space for school buildings. As you explore the problems facing one Florida school district, you will see the same issues that people around the world face everyday. Growing populations – of students, of community residents, and of populations in general – put stresses on our resources. This forces us to make decisions about which resources to consume and which to protect.

You will revisit the issues of growing populations and limited resources throughout the year. You will learn about communities having trouble finding water. You will learn about communities building new power plants to generate energy. You will also learn about communities that simply don't have enough space for their residents who need houses, roads, and schools.

In this chapter:

In this chapter, you will be introduced to a Florida school district that needs to make a decision about building a new school. You will read a letter from the school board president describing the overcrowding problems in their high school. You will look at the proposed location for the new school. Most important, you will think about how the school district could best use the land to relieve their overcrowding situation.

When you're done you'll be able to:

- Describe the overcrowding problem in the Florida school district.
- Determine if the proposed site for the new school can meet the needs of both the students and the district.

Overcrowded?

Essential Question: *What does the problem at Central High have to do with the environment?*

Overview

Read the following letter and answer the analysis questions with your class.

Letter

John Smiley
School Board President

Dear Students,

As members of the Parent, Teacher, and Student Association of the Central School District in Florida, we need your input on the following decision. As I'm sure you are aware, Central High School has become overcrowded, with over 200 students currently being taught in temporary classrooms. This population pressure is only going to get worse, as the school board predicts that we will have an additional 1000 students in the district within the next two years. In order to handle this problem and prevent similar ones in the future, we would like to build a school that can handle 2000 students total.

The piece of land that we have been given for the school site is home to 80 gopher tortoises, which are listed as a species of special concern in Florida. These tortoises are important to the upland ecosystem in Florida, and the school board does not want to wipe out this population of tortoises. Instead, we would like to create a plan that will allow the tortoises to co-exist on the site with the school. We think this will be an invaluable opportunity for science classes to observe the tortoises and we will be doing our part to preserve Florida's unique animals.

The total amount of land available is 100 acres. Approximately 4 acres are taken up by a river and 9 acres are on the far side of the river.

Your task is to determine where to place the school buildings to give us a good school, while still allowing the gopher tortoises to survive. Use the attached maps and building plans from the architect to help you make your decision.

Sincerely,

John Smiley

Analysis Questions

1. Why does the school district need a new high school?
2. Why do you think the school board wants to protect the tortoises? Do you think it is a good idea?
3. How do you think the tortoises will affect your decision about where to place the buildings?
4. Answer the essential question: *What does the problem at Central High have to do with the environment?*

Using Land Well

Essential Question: *Is the chosen piece of land appropriate for building a school?*

Procedure

Based on the letter you just read, use the map and building pieces on the next page to determine the best location for the school. Consider the desire of the school board to protect the tortoises and the ideal placement of the buildings for students.

Discussion Questions

1. Why did you choose the location that you did?
2. Was it a difficult decision? Why?
3. What information do you wish you had to allow you to make a better decision?
4. Answer the essential question: *Is the chosen piece of land appropriate for building a school?*

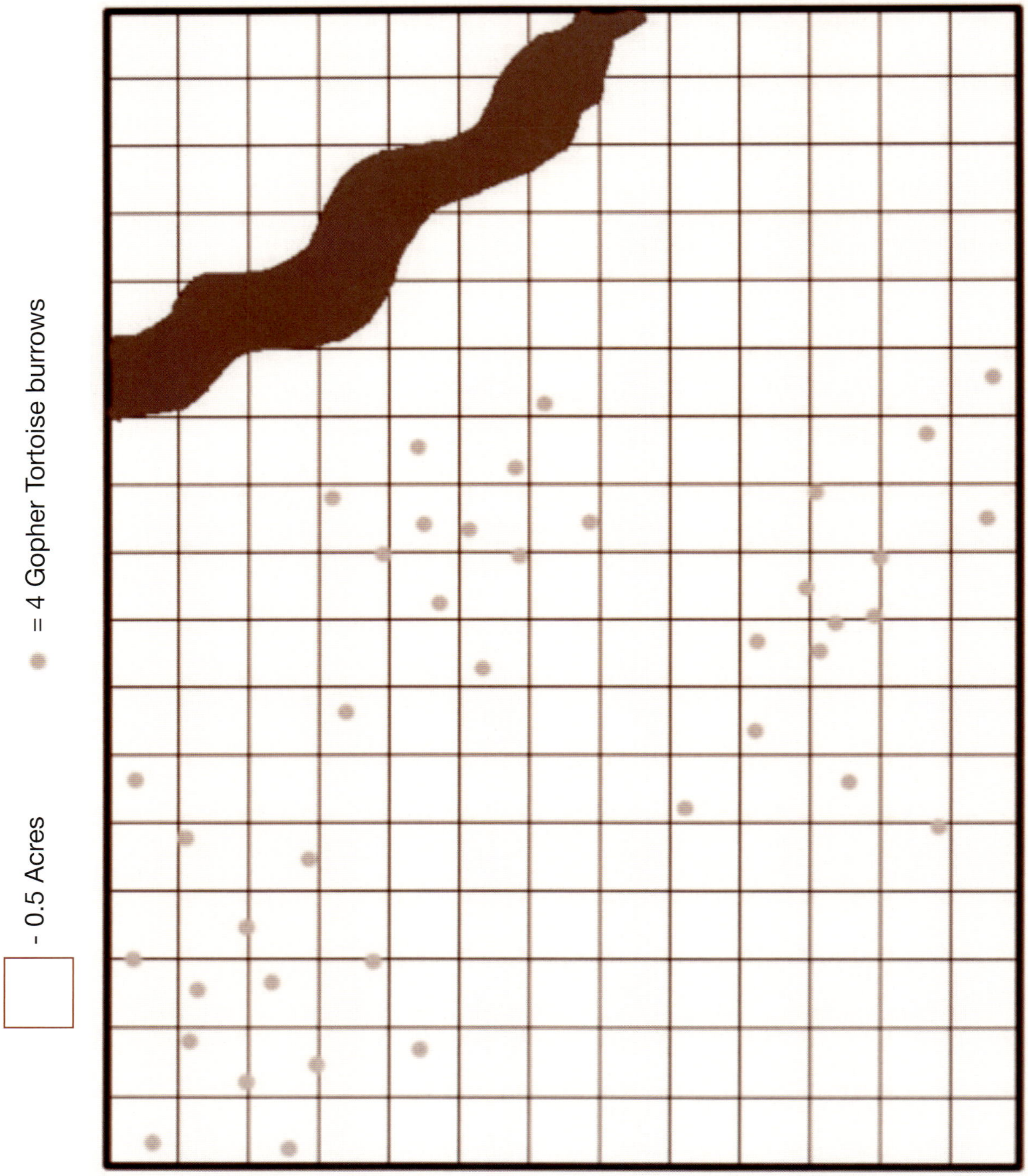
- 0.5 Acres
= 4 Gopher Tortoise burrows

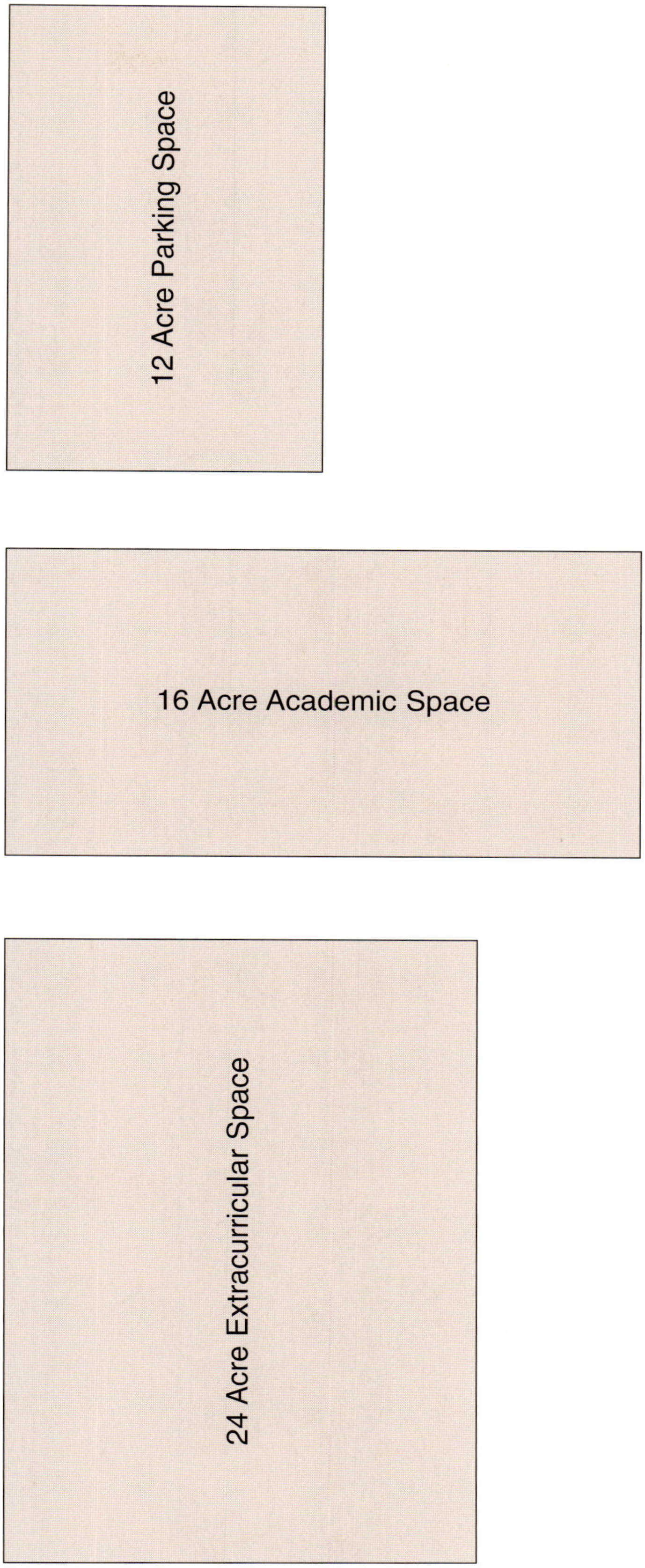

Figure 1: New School Building Pieces

CHAPTER 2

Populations

Chapter 2 Populations

Connections

The situation you read about in Chapter One is a familiar story for many students in the United States. School overcrowding, new building plans, and predictions of future growth are common problems in many school districts. Have you ever wondered why this is happening? Why are there so many new students in our schools?

In this chapter, you will explore population trends. Global population trends are important to understand because as populations grow, people consume more resources and need more land, water, and energy. The ability to predict future populations can help us make better decisions about everyday issues. A growing population often requires new schools and power plants and searching for new sources of water. Communities with a decreasing or stable population face different issues. In the next chapter, you will look at the availability of the resources that changing populations need and focus on current and future consumption.

In this chapter:

This chapter explores the changes in Earth's human population. Globally, human populations are growing. The reasons for the growth go back thousands of years to the development of agriculture. Advances in technology then enabled food and other resources to be transported over long distances. As a result, human populations started growing rapidly. As you study patterns of change in human populations, you will look at some examples of animal populations. You will see how they grow and shrink based on the resources available to them. You will look at trends in population growth from the past and predict future population trends. You will also explore the differences in population growth in the world, the United States, and your own community.

When you're done you'll be able to:

- Project the future population of a region given its birth and death rates.
- Interpret a population pyramid to predict the future growth or decline of a population.
- Analyze the sustainability of a population.

Lesson 1
What is a Population?

Driving Question: *What are the characteristics of our class population? Our Daphnia populations?*

Overview

In this lesson, you will look at two different populations: the population of small water fleas called *Daphnia*, and the population of your class and their families. You will start out in the laboratory, looking at a population of *Daphnia*. You will count the number of *Daphnia* in your sample and make sure they have enough food and water to survive. Each day for the next week, you will count the *Daphnia* and observe how the population grows and changes. You will also explore your family history to see how the population of your family has changed over several generations. You will combine your information with your classmates' to see how the population of your community has changed over time. In the next lesson, you will compare your class data to national and global population trends.

Important Content

- Populations depend on limited resources to survive.
- Unchecked growth can lead to an imbalance between a population and the resources that support it.
- Immigration, urbanization, and social and economic factors all affect human population growth.

Daphnia

Essential Question: *Describe how the population of Daphnia changes over time when grown in a closed system.*

Overview

A population is defined as a group of individuals from the same species that occupy the same space. In this activity, you will be observing an aquatic population of *Daphnia. Daphnia* are small aquatic crustaceans that live in freshwater ponds, lakes, and slow-moving streams. Their primary food is algae (tiny water plants), but they also feed on bacteria in the water. In this investigation, you will observe a sample of *Daphnia* for several days and graph the population of *Daphnia*. You will also calculate the net population growth rate and compare your results with those of your classmates.

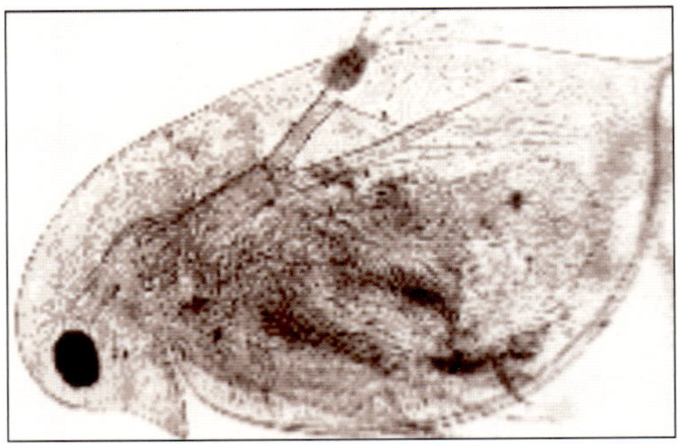

Figure 1: ***Daphnia***

Materials

For each class:
- 1 *Daphnia* culture

For each group:
- 1 magnifying glass
- graph paper
- grease pencil
- 1 clear 250 mL beaker
- 1 clear 50 mL beaker
- 1 3 mL pipette

Safety Concerns

Wear eye protection, clean up any spills or glassware breakage immediately.

Procedure

1. Make a prediction. Do you think your *Daphnia* population will increase, decrease, or stay the same? Record your prediction.
2. Start your *Daphnia* culture according to your teacher's instructions.
3. Mark the water level in the *Daphnia* culture container using the grease pencil. Maintain the water level according to your teacher's instructions.
4. Observe the *Daphnia* for 10 minutes. Record your observations on a separate sheet of paper. Draw a picture of the *Daphnia* that you see.

5. On a separate sheet, construct a data table with three columns labeled **date**, **total population of my *Daphnia*,** and **total population of *Daphnia* in the class**.
6. Count the number of *Daphnia* in your sample. Record the information in your data table. Return your sample to the location picked by your teacher.
7. Record the total number of *Daphnia* observed in your class. Repeat this process each day assigned by your teacher.

Counting the Daphnia in large numbers:

Use the following method when the *Daphnia* become too numerous to count. Obtain a 3 mL pipette, an empty 250 mL container, and an empty 50 mL container from your teacher. Using the pipette, transfer a 3 mL sample of your *Daphnia* to the small container. *Caution*: Don't expose the *Daphnia* to air. The air could get trapped in the *Daphnia's* shell, causing the *Daphnia* to rise to the surface and die. Record the number of *Daphnia* in the 3 mL sample. Carefully transfer the *Daphnia* to the 250 mL container. Obtain another 3 mL sample and repeat the process until all of the *Daphnia* have been recorded. Carefully transfer the *Daphnia* from the 250 mL container to the culture container. Return your sample to the location picked by your teacher.

Analysis Questions

1. Graph the population of your *Daphnia* and your class' *Daphnia* during the study period. Put the date on the x-axis and the number of *Daphnia* on the y–axis.
2. Compare your group's graph with others in your class. What are the similarities? What are the differences? Explain the differences between your graph and the graph of other groups.
3. Make a list of the variables you think might have affected the population of your *Daphnia*.
4. Why did you have to add water to your *Daphnia* sample? What evidence do you have to support your answer?
5. Based on your graph of population, what can you conclude about how *Daphnia* grow?
6. Answer the essential question: *Describe how the population of Daphnia changes over time when grown in a closed system.*

Personal Census Form

Essential Question: *Where did your relatives come from? Where did they move to in order to arrive where they are today?*

Overview

In this chapter, you will be studying populations of people on Earth, of *Daphnia* in the lab, and other examples. You will start by taking a personal census to look at your own family population. Did older generations have more brothers and sisters than you? Did they immigrate to this country? After you gather information about your family, you will combine it with your classmates' data. You should be able to see patterns in family size and determine family migration patterns. This information will help you understand how populations on Earth have changed over the years.

Procedure

Fill out as much as you can of the following chart. Choose one member of the generation older than you (a parent, an older relative or guardian). Then follow the generations back from that person. This information will be used only for class data analysis, but try to be as specific as possible. Be sure to indicate whether the locations of birth and current residence are rural areas (sparsely populated, mostly farmland), suburban areas (not as populated as cities, usually located near a major city), or urban areas (densely populated cities). Be sure to count all siblings (brothers and sisters), even those who may have died at a young age.

Analysis Question

1. Write a story that answers the essential question and describes what has happened to your ancestors over the generations.

Family Member	Number of Siblings	Birthplace (City, State, and Country)	Place of Most Recent Residence (City, State, and Country)	If Immigrated to USA, Approximate Year of Immigration
Me		☐ Urban ☐ Suburban ☐ Rural	☐ Urban ☐ Suburban ☐ Rural	
One Generation Older (Parent)		☐ Urban ☐ Suburban ☐ Rural	☐ Urban ☐ Suburban ☐ Rural	
Two Generations Older (Grandparent)		☐ Urban ☐ Suburban ☐ Rural	☐ Urban ☐ Suburban ☐ Rural	
Three Generations Older (Great-Grandparent)		☐ Urban ☐ Suburban ☐ Rural	☐ Urban ☐ Suburban ☐ Rural	

Census Analysis

Essential Question: *Do you think the trends in our classroom are typical for everyone in the United States? Why or why not?*

Overview

In this activity, you are going to look at census data gathered by the class. These data will be used to examine factors that affect populations more closely.

Procedure

Record the census data of your classmates on the Class Census Data Table.

1. Tally the number of rural, urban, and suburban birthplaces for (a) students, (b) one generation older, (c) two generations older, and (d) three generations older. (Room for 32 classmates is included.)
2. Tally the number of rural, urban, and suburban residences for (a) students, (b) one generation older, (c) two generations older, and (d) three generations older.
3. Tally the number of siblings for (a) students, (b) one generation older, (c) two generations older, and (d) three generations older.
4. Make three bar graphs of the class data: one graph for births, one for siblings, and the other for residences. Be sure to place the categories on the *x*–axis and totals on the *y*–axis.

Analysis Questions

1. Look at the class data on the number of siblings you observe. What patterns do you see? (For example, is there an increase or decrease in the number of children and siblings born from the oldest to the youngest generation?)
2. What factors do you think influenced this pattern?
3. Look at class data on urban, suburban, and rural population. What patterns do you see?
4. What factors do you think influenced these patterns?
5. Based on the numbers in your class, when did most of our ancestors immigrate to the United States?
6. Answer the essential question: *Do you think the trends in our classroom are typical for everyone in the United States? Why or why not?*

Data Table 1: Birthplace

	Student			One Generation Older			Two Generations Older			Three Generations Older		
Classmate	Urban	Suburban	Rural	Urban	Suburban	Rural	Urban	Suburban	Rural	Urban	Suburban	Rural
1												
2												
3												
4												
5												
6												
7												
8												
9												
10												
11												
12												
13												
14												
15												
16												
17												
18												
19												
20												
21												
22												
23												
24												
25												
26												
27												
28												
29												
30												
31												
32												
Total												

Data Table 2: Recent Residence

	Student			One Generation Older			Two Generations Older			Three Generations Older		
Classmate	Urban	Suburban	Rural	Urban	Suburban	Rural	Urban	Suburban	Rural	Urban	Suburban	Rural
1												
2												
3												
4												
5												
6												
7												
8												
9												
10												
11												
12												
13												
14												
15												
16												
17												
18												
19												
20												
21												
22												
23												
24												
25												
26												
27												
28												
29												
30												
31												
32												
Total												

Data Table 3: Number of Siblings

Classmate	Student	One Generation older	Two Generations older	Three Generations older
1				
2				
3				
4				
5				
6				
7				
8				
9				
10				
11				
12				
13				
14				
15				
16				
17				
18				
19				
20				
21				
22				
23				
24				
25				
26				
27				
28				
29				
30				
31				
32				
Total				

Lesson 2
Looking at Populations in ArcView

Driving Question: *How can computer software help us learn about the world around us?*

Overview

You have some information about how your community's population has changed over the years. Now you will explore national and global populations. One tool that can help you study population is a computer program called ArcView. In this lesson, you will use ArcView to learn about world population and U.S. population growth. You will use ArcView throughout the year as you study different aspects of environmental science.

Basic ArcView Skills

Essential Question: *What kind of information can we get from ArcView?*

Overview

ArcView allows you to look at information based on its geographic location. You often see information displayed this way in TV or newspaper weather maps.

In this lesson, you will learn basic ArcView skills, including working with views and themes, and zooming.

As you go through these activities, use the Lesson 2*: ArcView Tip Sheet* to keep track of the buttons you learn to use.

Portions of this activity were adapted with permission from "A Quick Guide to Viewing Data With ArcView GIS 3.x" by Bob Coulter of the Missouri Botanical Gardens, St. Louis, MO.

Materials

For each group:

- ArcView software
- Populations.apr project

Figure 1: Project Window

Procedure

1. Open the ArcView project Population.apr according to your teacher's instructions.

Part 1: Working with Views and Themes

Figure 2: Hide/Show Legend

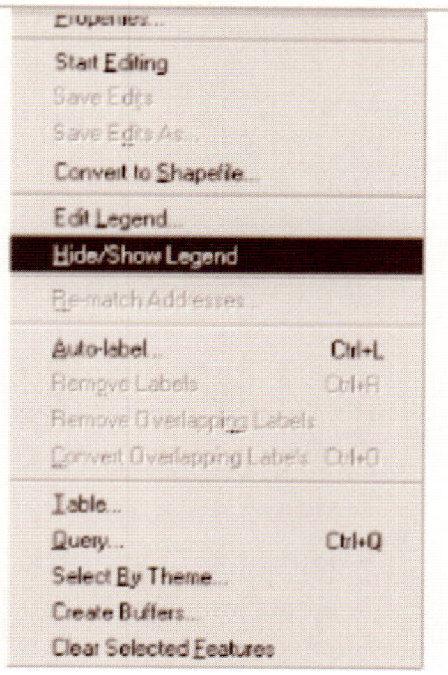

2. You should be looking at the Project Window, which lists Views, Tables, Charts, and Layouts. Today, you will learn about Views. Double click the View named Intro.
3. A View includes layers of geographic information for a place or region. Each layer is a collection of geographic features such as states, roads, or cities. In the View for this project, the themes (listed on the left) represent different information about these features. Click the check boxes next to States.shp and Counties.shp to turn on those themes. Notice how the Counties theme covers the States theme.
4. Under the theme name, there is a legend for that theme. You can hide or show a legend using the Theme menu at the top center of the screen. To do this, click once on the theme name for States.shp (not the check box you just clicked on). This makes the theme active, and it will appear highlighted or slightly raised in its appearance in the table of contents. Then, go to the Theme menu and choose Hide/Show Legend.

5. The legend for States.shp shows a different color for each state. The legend for counties is different. It shows different shades of red to show the population of the county. Darker red means a larger population. Colors and symbols in ArcView reveal information about a location. The legend is a guide to understand those colors and symbols. How many counties do you observe with a population greater than 3,000,000?

6. Turn on the Cities.shp theme.

7. The theme at the top of the list appears on top of the other themes in the view. To rearrange this order, click and drag the theme names into the order you want. Arrange the themes with cities on top, followed by counties and then states.

Figure 3: Cities, Counties and States of the United States

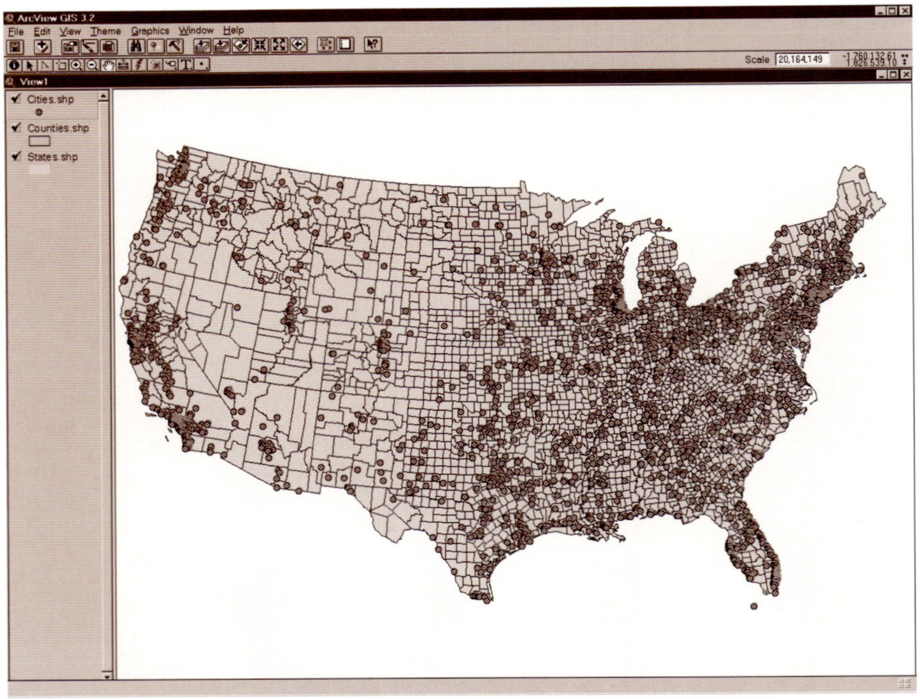

Practice

1. Close the Intro View and open the one called Practice.
2. Turn on Countries.shp and Worldcities.shp. (You may need to scroll down to see Worldcities.)
3. Hide the legend for Countries.shp.
4. Rearrange the themes so Worldcities is at the top.
5. Close the Practice View and open the Intro view to continue with the next section.

Part 2: Zooming In and Out

8. Turn off the Cities and States themes.

9. To zoom in on a specific area, select the Zoom In tool. (It looks like a magnifying glass with a plus sign.)

10. With that tool selected, you can now zoom in one of two ways. The simplest is to click repeatedly on the area you want enlarged until the map looks the way you want. This method is not very exact and it is slow. A better way is to select the Zoom In tool and draw a box around the area you want to zoom in on. Zoom in on Florida.

Figure 4: Zoom to full extent

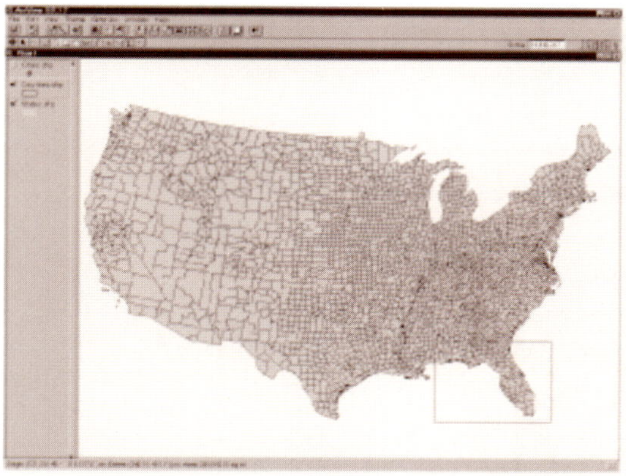

Figure 5: Zoom in on Florida

11. To look at a larger area, click on the Zoom Out button. (It looks like a magnifying glass with the minus sign): Click once on that button to select it and click the center of the map.

Figure 6: Zoom out

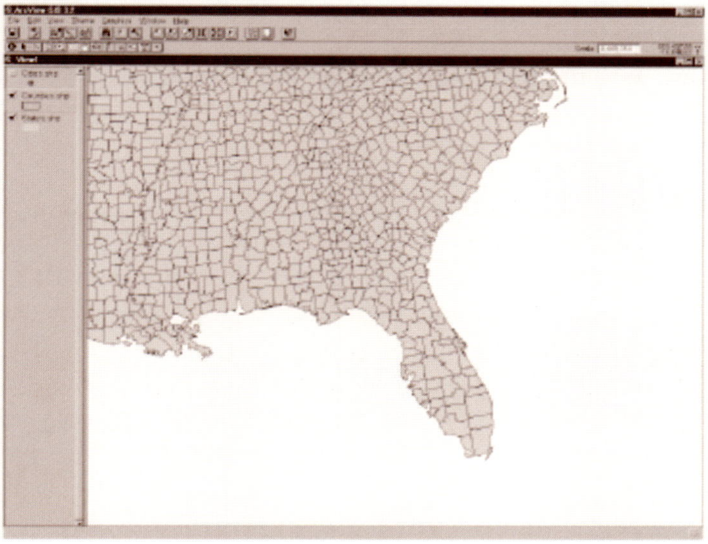

12. If you want to go back to the previous view, click the Zoom to Previous Extent button:

Figure 7: Zoom to previous extent button

13. If you're too far in or out, click the Zoom to Full Extent button.  This will take you back to the widest view needed to display all of your themes.

14. Zoom in on Florida again.

15. If you need to slide the map just a bit more, use the Pan tool by clicking once on the pan button.  Click anywhere on the map, hold the mouse button down, and slide the map into position. Slide the map to see New England.

Figure 8: Move to New England area

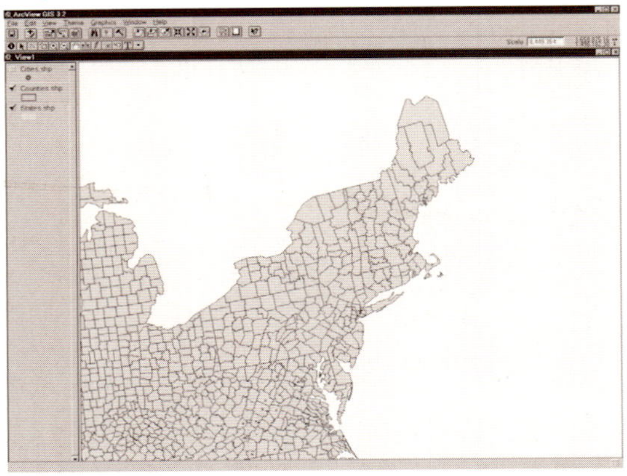

Practice

1. Zoom to Full Extent.
2. Zoom in on California.
3. Zoom out and slide the map until you can see from California east to Texas.
4. Zoom to Full Extent.
5. Return to Previous Extent of California to Texas.
6. Zoom to Full Extent.

16. To close an ArcView project, click the X in the upper right corner of the Project Window. You can also go to the File menu and select Close Project. Do not save unless instructed to by your teacher.

17. To quit the program, click the X in the upper right corner of your screen or select Exit from the File menu.

18. Answer the essential question: *What kind of information can we get from ArcView?*

Advanced ArcView Skills

Essential Question: *How do queries help us find information faster?*

Overview

Querying is asking ArcView to answer a question based on the data in the themes. You can ask questions like: Which cities have a population greater than 10 million? Which states are larger than 4000 square miles? As you get more comfortable with queries, you can combine them to answer more complex questions like: Which cities with a population greater than 2 million have more women than men living in them?

Use Lesson 2: *ArcView Tip Sheet* to help you with new buttons and error messages.

Materials

For each group:
- ArcView software
- Populations.apr project

Procedure

Part 1: The Query Function

1. Open the project Populations.apr and the view Intro.
2. Turn on the theme Counties.shp
3. You are going to query for counties with high population densities. With the Counties.shp theme active, click the Query Builder button.
4. In the window that appears, make sure the Update Values box is checked. This ensures that you are querying the data that presently exists in the theme's table.
5. On the left is a list of Fields. Scroll down the list until you see Pop90_sqmi (population per square mile in 1990). Double click this field. Pop90_sqmi s hould now appear in the window below the Fields list.
6. Next, select large values by clicking the Greater Than button once.

Figure 1: Query - Population that is greater than 810 people per square mile

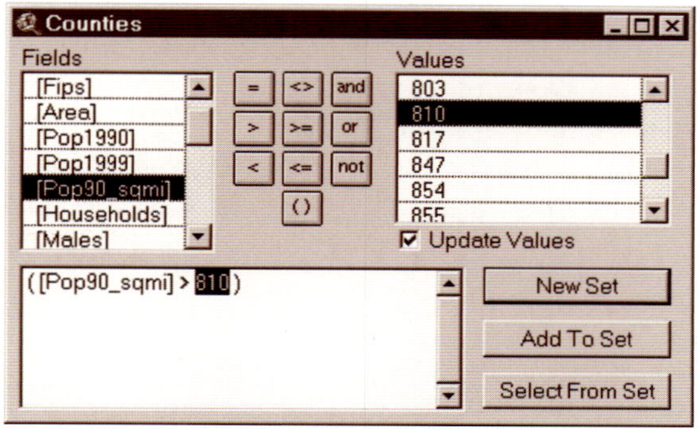

7. In the Values field, scroll down until you see 810 and double click. (You can also type 810 in the box.) You are selecting population per square mile that is greater than 810.

8. To have ArcView answer the query, click the New Set button.

9. ArcView now processes your query. You have just selected all the counties whose population density is greater the 810 people per square mile. These selections appear highlighted in yellow in the View. Close the query window.

10. Zoom in on Florida. Count the number of counties in Florida that have population density greater than 810. After you have done this, Zoom to Full Extent.

11. Next, you are going to find which of those counties have a larger Black population than White population. Start by clicking the Query Builder button with the counties theme active.

12. In the Fields list, scroll down until you find the White field and double click it. That field should now appear in the Query box below the Fields list.

13. Choose the Less Than operator button for the counties whose White population is less then the Black population. In the Fields list, scroll down until you see Black and double click it.

14. Press the Select From Set button. This will select from the set you already created. You will see a selection of counties highlighted in yellow. These are the counties, which have a higher Black than White population and a population density greater then 810. Close the query window and zoom to the east coast to find the counties.

15. Clear the selected features using the Clear Selected Features button.

Figure 2: Query - Find the areas where there are a greater number of black individuals in the population

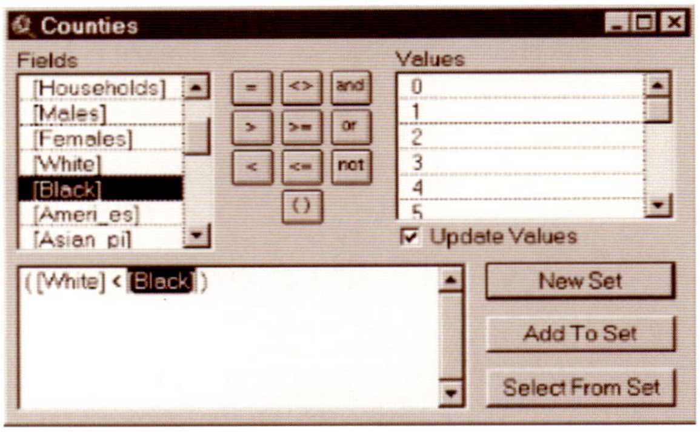

Practice

1. You should be zoomed in on the east coast.
2. Make States.shp the active theme and hide its legend.
3. Turn on the Cities theme and move it to the top of the theme list.
4. Click the Query Builder button.
5. Select the 1990 Population field, Greater Than button, and type 3000000.
6. Click New Set (one city should be highlighted in your view). Close the query window.
7. Clear the selection.
8. Query to find cities where Median Rent is greater than $700. (Median rent is the average cost of rent for the city you select.)
9. Find cities within that set (rent greater than $700) that also have elevation greater than 500.
10. Look in Illinois, near Chicago, to find three of them.

Part 2: The Identify Tool

16. Now you are going to find the names of the cities you just selected. You should still be zoomed in on Chicago.

17. Click the Identify Tool button. With the Cities theme active, click on a highlighted city. Information about the city will appear in a new window.

18. What is the name of the city you selected? What is the population of the city?

Figure 3: The Chicagoland area

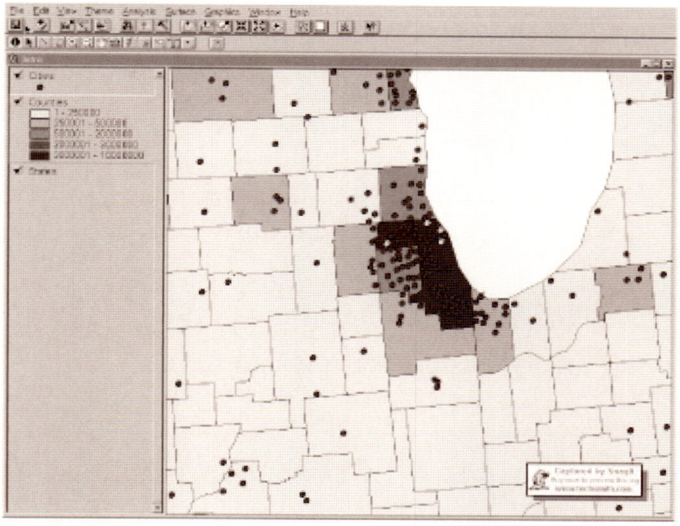

19. Next, you are going to find the name of the county that city is located in. Turn on the counties theme and make it active.

20. Using the Identify Tool, find the name of county that city is in.

Part 3: Theme Tables

21. Another way to find the items you've selected is in the theme table. The theme table contains all of the information about a theme. You can look at it by clicking the Theme Table button while the Cities theme is active. You'll see a table of information.

22. The items you selected (cities with rent greater than $700 and elevation greater than 500) are highlighted yellow in the table. To find the items faster, click the Promote button. This will bring all the selected items to the top of the table. How many items are selected?

23. Clear the selection. Close the theme table. Zoom to Full Extent.

Figure 4: Cities table

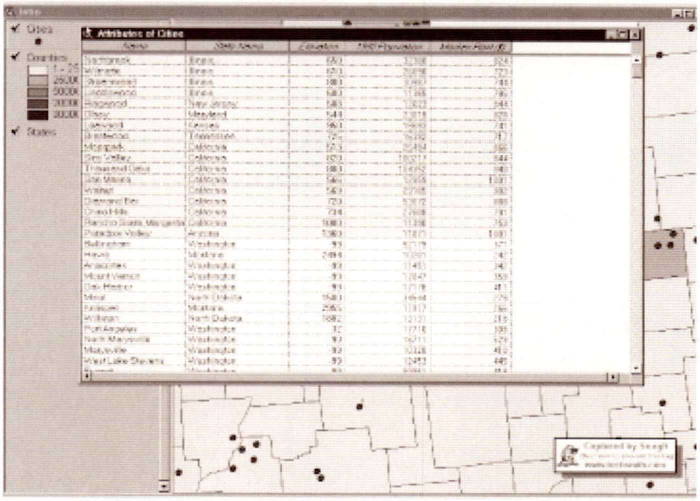

Practice – Exploring Population Growth

1. Use the query tool to find counties where the population in 1999 is greater than the population in 1990. In most counties, did population grow from 1990 to 1999?
2. Clear the selection and query for states where population has gone down between 1990 and 1999. (*Hint:* If you have trouble seeing which states are selected, use the theme table to get a list of states.) Which states had a population drop between 1990 and 1999?
3. Find Florida. Write down the 1990 and 1999 population of each.
4. Find your home county and state. Write down the 1990 and 1999 population of each.

Analysis Questions

1. In general, has the population of the U.S. been growing or shrinking? What did you see in ArcView to prove this?
2. Did the population in Florida grow or shrink from 1990 to 1999? What about your home county? Your home state?
3. Why do you think this is happening? Use information from your census forms in Lesson 1 to think of reasons.
4. Think of a question about populations that you could answer with ArcView. Write the question, the procedure you would use to find the answer, and the answer. Trade questions with another group of students, and see if you can answer their question.
5. Answer the essential question: *How do queries help us find information faster?*

More ArcView Practice

Essential Question: *Where are the largest cities in the world located?*

Procedure

1. Open Populations.apr and the view Practice.

2. Turn on the Countries.shp theme to view the countries of the world. Hide the legend.

3. Turn on the Worldcities.shp theme. Rearrange the themes so Worldcities.shp is on top.

4. Query the cities data to find the biggest cities in the world. With the Worldcities theme active, click the Query Builder button. From the Fields list, select Population and double click. Next, choose the Greater Than operator button. Type in 15000000 (no commas) and click New Set.

Figure 1: Query - Find the places in the world where the population is greater than 1,500,000

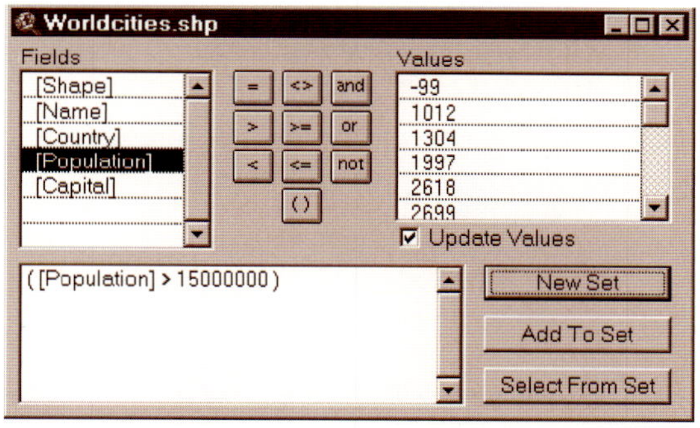

5. Zoom in on Japan.

6. In the toolbar, click the Identify button. Click on the highlighted cities and record the names.

7. After you have recorded the names, Zoom to Full Extent.

Figure 2: Zoom in on Japan

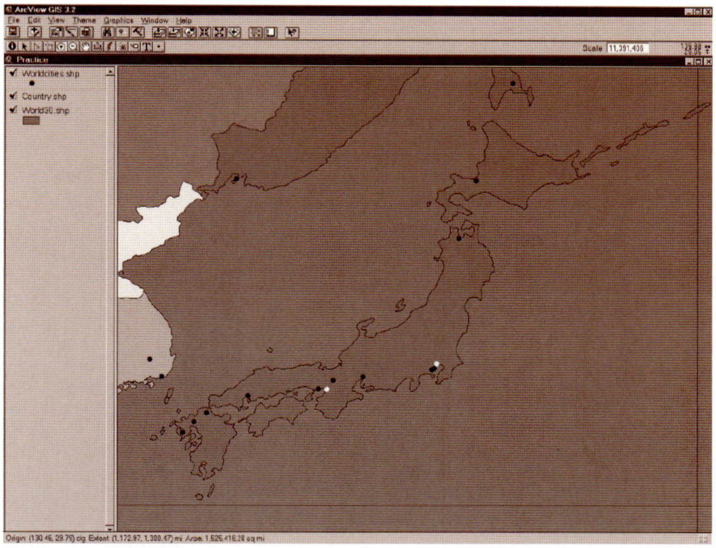

Practice

1. Name three cities in Italy with a population greater than 2 million.

2. Find three countries with populations greater than 80 million and areas (sq_mile_cntry) less than 150000.

3. In the Intro view, find two counties with an area greater than 7000 and an American Eskimo population less than 100.

ArcView Tip Sheet

Essential Question: *What ArcView commands will you need to remember the next time you use the program?*

Use this sheet to keep track of commands in ArcView. Add your own notes as you learn more about the program.

1. To **turn a theme on** (make it appear on the map), click the check box next to its name in the table of contents. In this example, cities would appear on the map but states would not.

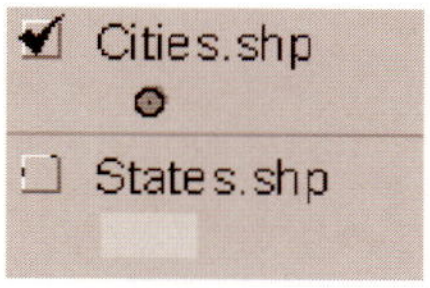

2. To **turn a theme off**, uncheck the box.
3. To make a theme **active,** click on the name of the theme. It should look raised or highlighted. You must make a theme active to do a query, clear a selection, show/hide the legend, etc.
4. To **rearrange the order** of the themes, click on the theme name you want to move and drag it into the place you wish.
5. To **zoom in**, use the Zoom In button.  Select the Zoom tool and drag a box around the area you wish to look at more closely.
6. To **zoom out** from where you are, use the Zoom Out button  and click on the center of the map.
7. The Back button  takes you to the **last view** you had.
8. The Zoom to Full Extent button  zooms out to **see the whole map**.
9. To **move the map** within the view window, use the Pan tool.  Click on the screen and drag the map to where you want it.
10. Use the Identify Tool  to **see information** about a feature.
11. Use the Theme Table button  to **view the table of information** about a theme.
12. Use the Promote button  to **bring selected features to the top** of the list.
13. To clear a selection, click the **Clear Selected Features** button .

14. Use the Query Builder button  to **build queries** and make selections.

In the query dialogue, double click the records in the Fields and Values lists:

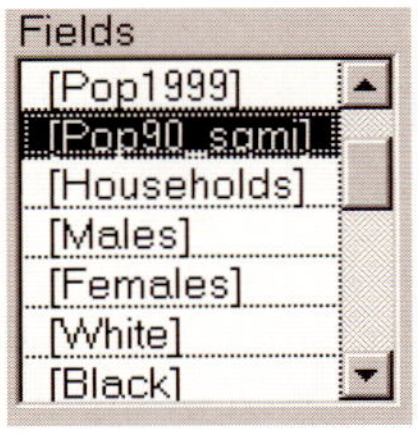

Single click the operator buttons:

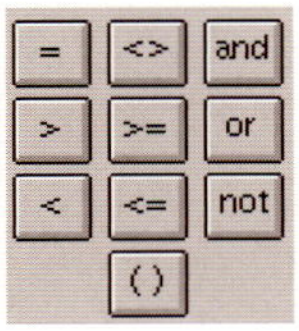

Select [New Set] for new selections.

Select [Select From Set] to choose from within previous selections.

Common Problems

1. **The Identify tool gives the wrong information or will not give information.** Make sure the theme you want information about is active (highlighted) on the left. Make sure you are zoomed in far enough so it is clear what you are clicking on.

2. **The maps load very slowly.** Turn off all the themes you aren't using. ArcView re-draws each one every time you zoom in or out. Zoom in by drawing a square around the area you want to see instead of by clicking on the map.

3. **I get a syntax error when I make a query.** Queries should look like one of these:

   ([field] > 367000)

   ([field] < [field])

   ([field] = "text")

   Make sure there are parentheses at both ends of the query and brackets around field names. Numbers should have no commas, units or other symbols in them. Text should be in quotes (For example, a query for ([CountryName] = "France").

Lesson 3
Population Changes

Driving Question: *How are populations on Earth growing and changing?*

Overview

So far in this chapter, you have seen the changes in your own families and in U.S. population. While family size might be getting smaller, the population of the U.S. is getting larger. Why is this happening? What does it mean for future populations in our country?

In this lesson, you will look at the population of the world and see how it has grown over time. You will use a tool called population pyramids to see how looking at different age groups in a population can help you predict whether a population will grow or shrink. You will make similar predictions with birth rates and death rates. You will finish the lesson with calculations using birth and death rates. Understanding population changes will help you see why growing communities have needs like new schools. This will help you answer the question about what to do about the new school in Florida.

Important Content

- Earth's human population has been growing at an increasing rate in recent years.
- Immigration, urbanization, and socioeconomic factors all relate to human population growth in important ways.
- Birth rate and death rate are measurements used to determine population growth.

Distribution of Humans

***Essential Question**: How do historical references help to explain changes and trends in population?*

Overview

ArcView showed the U.S. population growing between 1990 and 1999. Similar things are happening all over the Earth and have been for many years. Today, you will watch a video to see how the Earth's population has changed. The video shows human population growth from 1 AD to the projected population in 2030.

Materials

For each class:
- World population video

Procedure

1. Watch the video the first time to see the changes in global population. Notice the time period reference in the bottom right-hand corner.
2. Watch the video again and record your observations. For example, write down historical references and dates when major population changes occurred.

Class Discussion Questions

1. Around what year did you begin to notice a large increase in population growth?
2. What historical events, scientific advances, or other changes at that time may have contributed to the population increase?
3. Were there any points in the film when you noticed a slight decrease in the population? If so, in what part(s) of the world did you notice a decreasing population?
4. What historical events at that time may have contributed to the population decreases?
5. On the next page, there is a map of Earth's current population density. (Population density is the number of organisms in a particular population per square unit of area.) You will use the map in the next chapter when you study Earth resources. Based on the video, mark a few areas on the map where you think population is growing the fastest.
6. Answer the essential question: *How do historical references help to explain changes and trends in population?*

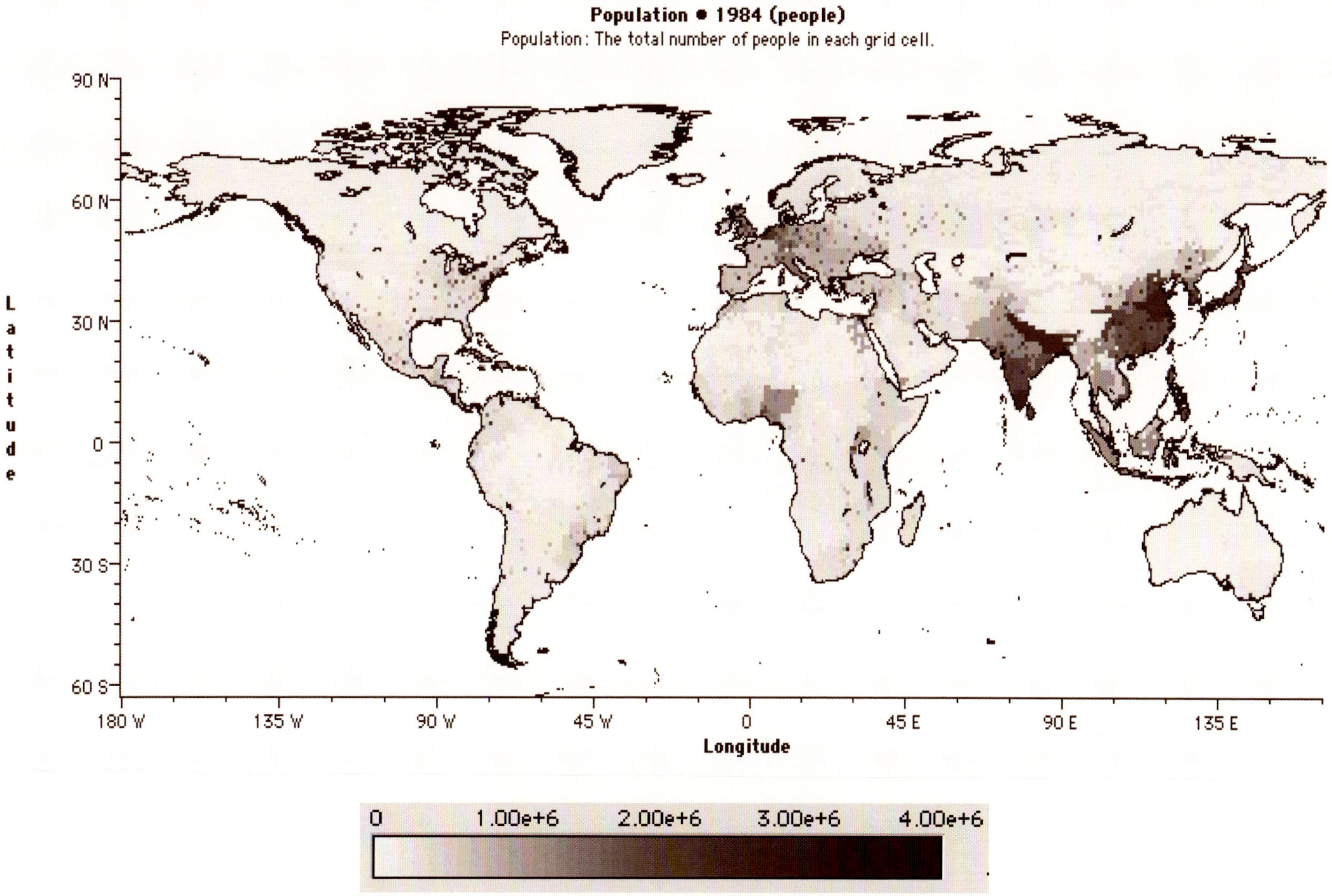

Figure 1: Human Population Around The World in 1984

You will use this map again in Chapter 3: Resources.

Population Growth

Essential Question: *What will the world's population be in 2100?*

Overview

In the last activity, you saw a video showing the world's population growth over time. As of 1999, the world's population reached 6 billion. It has surpassed that number today. How did our population become so large? Is the world's population increasing at a steady rate? To answer these questions, you will calculate population growth rates using world population data.

Population growth rates (PGR) show a percentage of change in the population over a given time. The PGR reflects the emigration and immigration into a given area and the total number of births and deaths in that area during a period of time. The population growth rate gives scientists a better picture of population trends.

In this activity, you will determine the current world population growth rate and predict the population for 2100. Since you are using world population data, your PGR values will reflect only birth and death rates over a period of time.

Materials

For each group:
- graph paper
- ruler

Procedure

1. Make a line graph of the "World's Population" data shown on the next page.

   * *Note that the population value for the year 2050 is a projected number.*

2. Use the formula below to calculate the population growth rate (PGR) for the years 1800–2050.

   The PGR is calculated by the increase in the world's population during a specified time and divided by the population at the start of that specified time.

$$\frac{\text{Current Year} - \text{Previous Year}}{\text{Previous Year}} \times 100\% = \text{PGR}$$

   Example calculation to find the PGR for years 1800-1850:

$$\frac{1211 - 900}{900} \times 100\% = 35\%$$

Analysis Questions

1. What can you interpret from this graph?
2. Is the world's population growing at the same rate? Why or why not?
3. Can you think of a reason why the population won't keep growing as the graph predicts?
4. Use your graph to answer the essential question: *What will the world's population be in 2100?* Explain your reasoning.

World Population Growth

Year (AD)	**Population** (in Millions)
1	170
200	190
400	190
600	200
800	220
1000	265
1100	320
1200	360
1300	360
1400	350
1500	425
1600	545
1700	610
1750	760
1800	900
1850	1,211
1900	1,625
1950	2,515
2000	6,073
2050*	9,298

* *projected*

Population Pyramids

***Essential Question**: How do population pyramids help us predict future populations?*

Overview

Over time, human population has not stayed the same. There are periods of time where the population expands at rapid rates and there are times where the growth slows down. You saw this in the World Population graph you made for *Population Growth.* Why is this? Even though population on Earth is growing, we saw in ArcView that some states in the U.S. have declining populations. So where is population growing and where is it shrinking? Is there a way we can look at a current population and predict its future growth?

Today, you will look at a tool called population pyramids. Scientists use this tool to analyze populations and predict their growth. Population pyramids show population data for different age groups in a population.

Procedure

1. We will start by looking at the U.S. population in 1960, which is shown on the next page.
2. Females are on the right, males on the left, and the numbers in the center are ages. So the number of children aged 10-14 in 1960 was about 8.2 million girls and 8.3 million boys.

Stop and Think

How many women aged 45-49 were there in the U.S. in 1960?

What was the total number of people aged over 85 in the U.S. in 1960?

Data Table 1: United States population pyramid for 1960

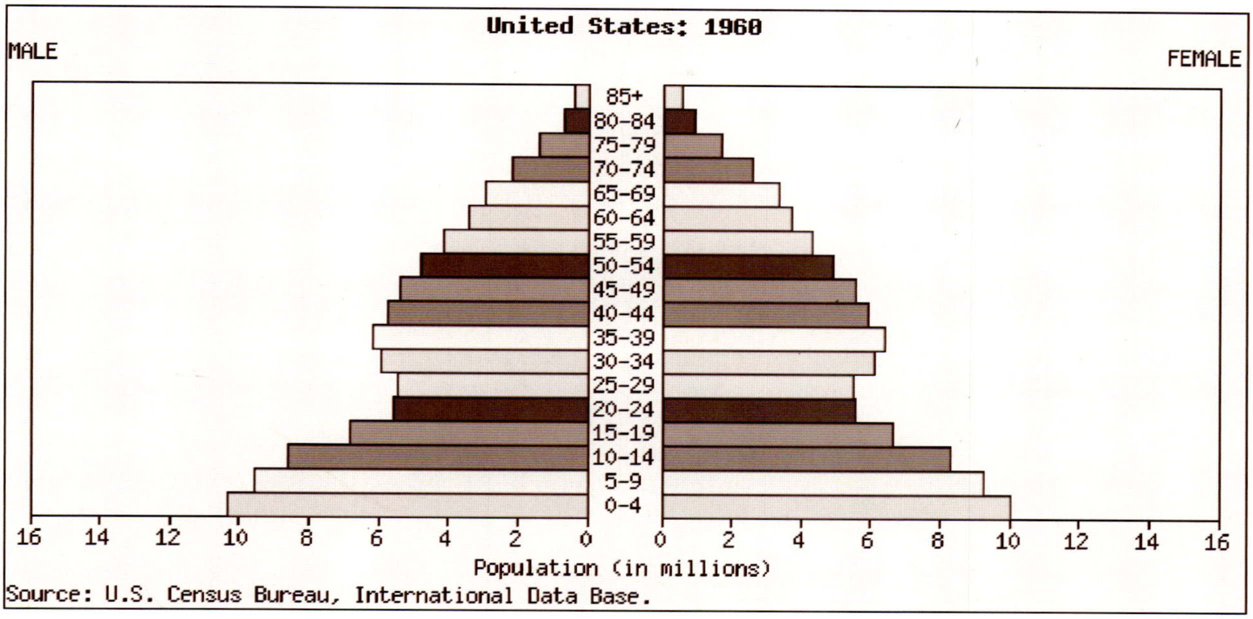

Data Table 2: United States population pyramid for 1980

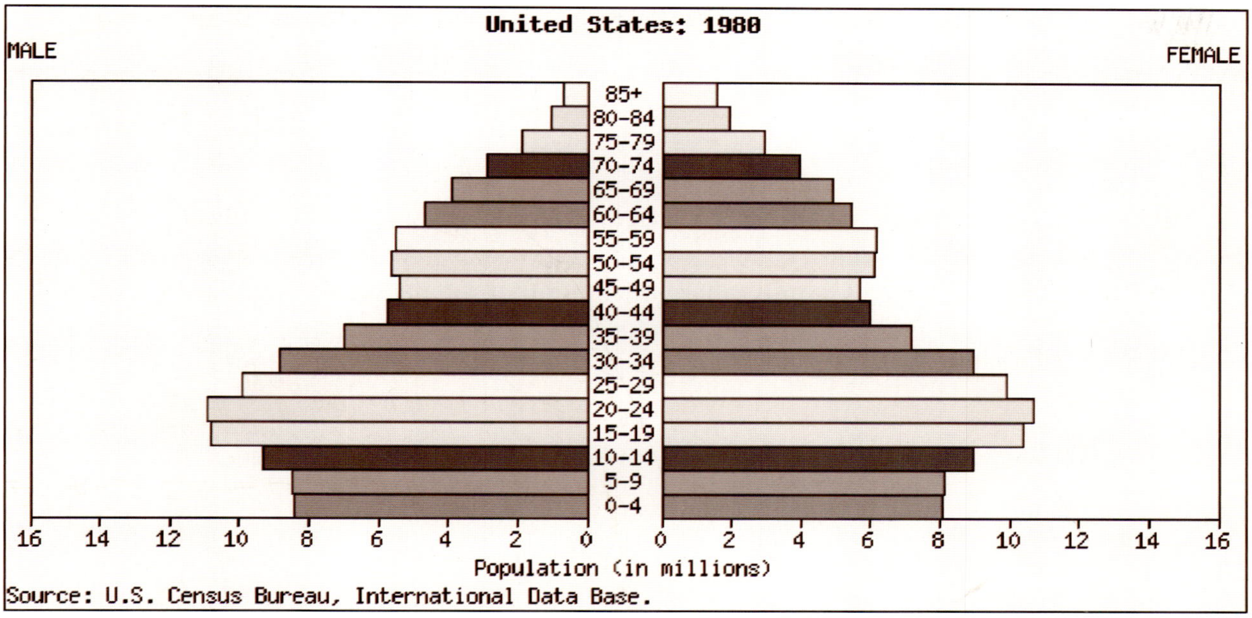

3. Compare the 1960 pyramid to 1980. In the 1960 pyramid, there are 10 million girls and about 11 million boys in the 0-4 age group. This generation of individuals is known as the "Baby Boom." In 1980, those kids grew up to be 20-24. (The amount over 10 million is due to immigration.)

4. The population of women aged 40-44 in 1960 dropped from about 5.9 million to 5.6 million in 1980 (when they were in the 60-64 age group). This is due to deaths from disease and old age.

Stop and Think

Suppose everyone got married at age 20 and started a family, and each family had two children. How many children would you expect there to be between 0 and 4 years old in 1980?

What would you expect if each family had only 1 child?

Data Table 3: United States population pyramid for 2000

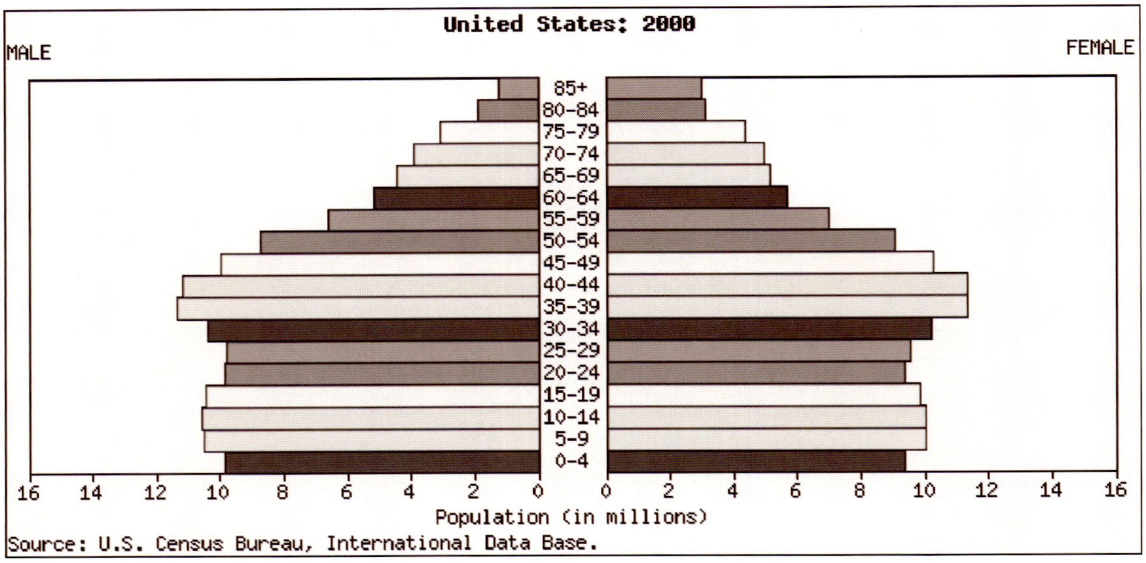

5. The population pyramid for the year 2000 in the U.S. is beginning to have almost straight sides. Many developed countries look this way. It indicates a more stable population. Some developed countries have pyramids where the bottom of the pyramid is smaller than the top. This indicates a population that is getting smaller. Other countries have pyramids that really look like pyramids. This shape indicates a population that is still growing rapidly.

Class Discussion Questions

Look at the pyramids on the next page to answer the following questions.

1. Describe what happened to the population of Belize between 1980 and 2000.
2. What would you expect the pyramid for Belize to look like in 2010?
3. The population pyramids for Taiwan 2050 and United States 2050 are predictions for the future. How do you think those predictions were made?
4. Compare the Taiwan and United States predictions for 2050. Which population is growing? Which is shrinking?
5. Explain the large number of people over age 85 in Taiwan and the United States in 2050. Why are there more women than men?

6. How would an increase in fertility and longer life spans affect the shape of a population pyramid?
7. Answer the essential question: *How do population pyramids help us predict future populations?*

Data Table 4: Belize population pyramid for 1980

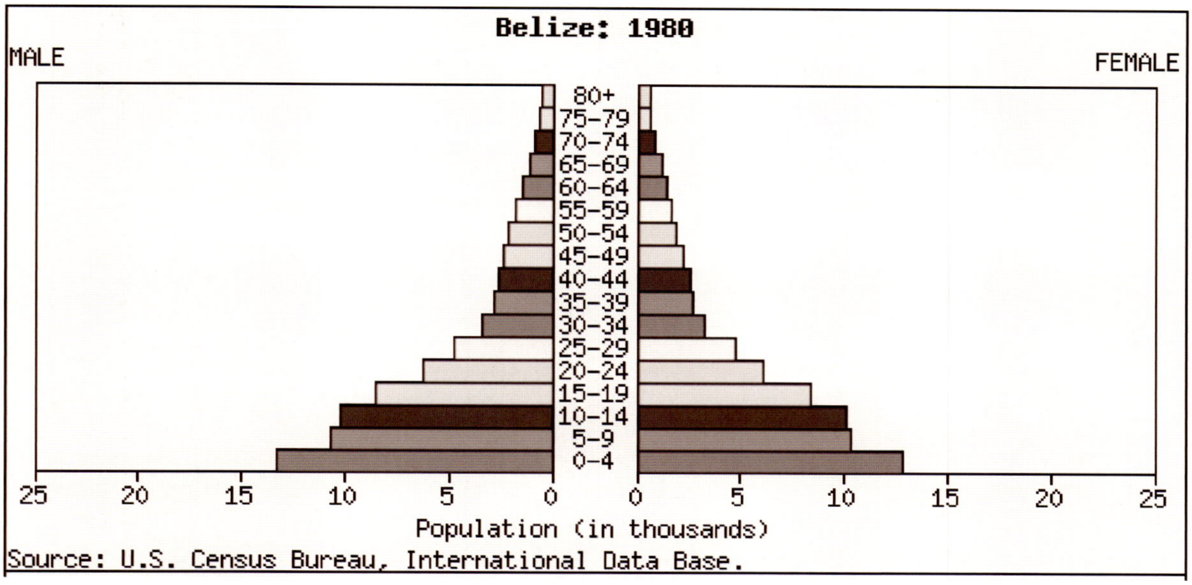

Data Table 4: Belize population pyramid for 2000

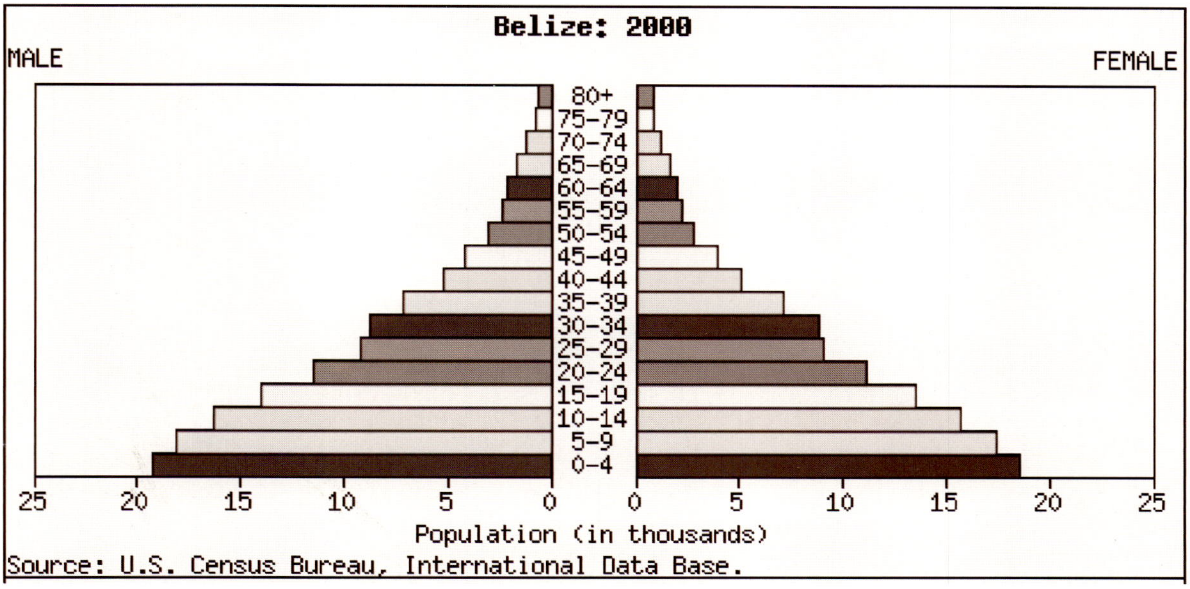

Data Table 6: United States projected population pyramid for 2050

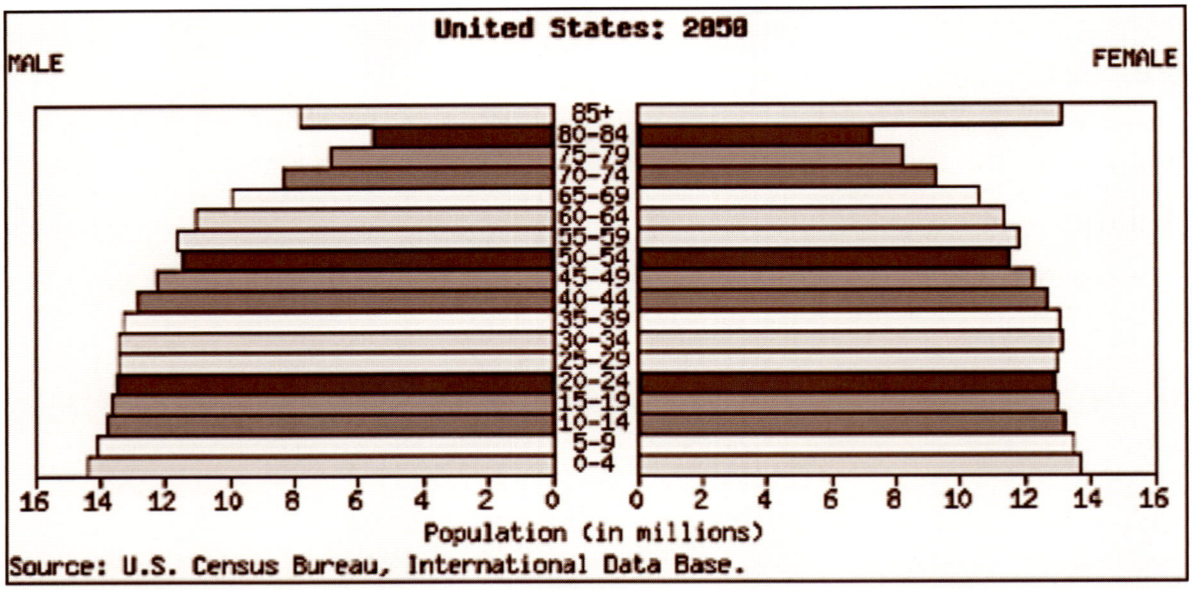

Data Table 7: Taiwan projected population pyramid for 2050

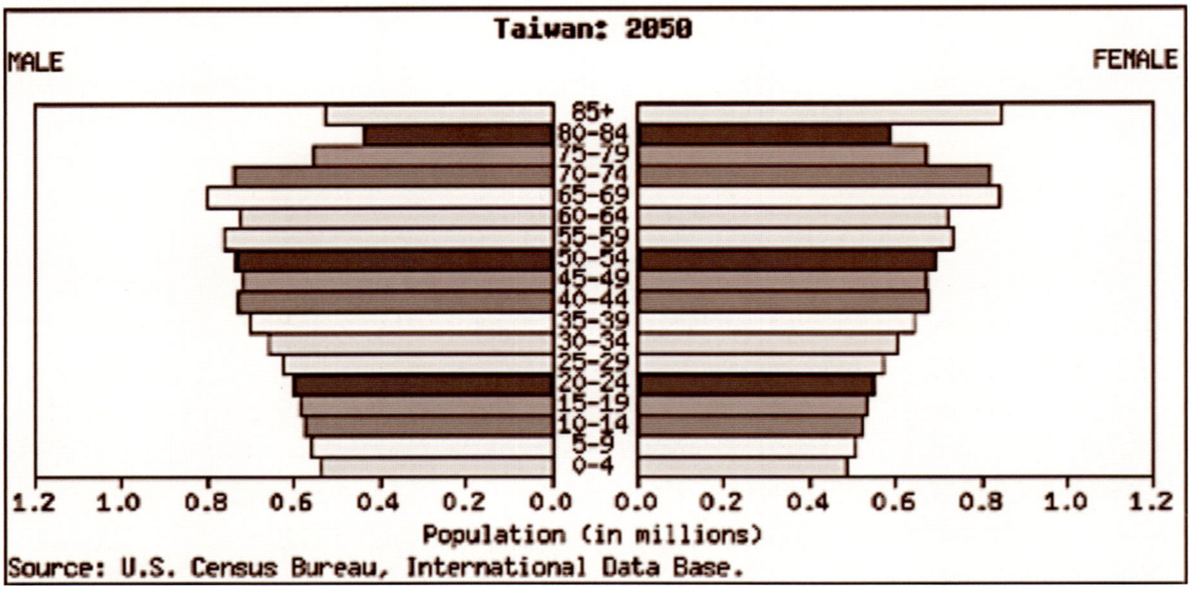

Paper Clip Creatures

Essential Question: *How do births and deaths affect the size of a population?*

Overview

In this activity, you will play a counting game with paper clips. Pretend that when two paper clips are connected, they become a living "paper clip creature." When paper clips are separated, the creature dies. In a fixed time period, called a "year," the "storks" in your group will try to give birth to as many paper clip creatures as possible by fastening paper clips together. At the same time, the "grim reapers" will try to destroy as many paper clip creatures as possible by separating paper clips.

Materials

For each group:
- 1 empty pie tin or pie pan
- 1 box of 100 jumbo paper clips
- 1 stopwatch

Safety Concerns

When finished, return all materials as instructed by your teacher.

Procedure

Part 1

1. In your group of five, assign the following roles: two storks, two grim reapers, and one timer.
2. Count the number of unconnected paper clips and write the number in Data Table 1 by year 0. There should be no living paper clip creatures (connected paper clips) at the beginning.
3. The timer should announce "start" and amount of time for a "year." For this activity, a year will last 30 seconds. Storks should try to fasten together as many paper clips as possible and return the pairs to the pile. Grim Reapers should try to separate as many paper clips as possible. Continue working until the time runs out.
4. Count the number of living paper clip creatures and unconnected paper clips in the pile. Record your results on the data table. Do not disconnect any connected paper clips at this time.
5. Repeat Steps 3 and 4 until you have run five years total.

Part 2

6. Disconnect all paper clips.
7. Your teacher will give different roles to each of your group members. Record the number of storks and grim reapers on Data Table 2. Also record the number of unconnected paper clips for year 0.
8. Run five years total.

Analysis Questions

1. Make a graph of the number of paper clip creatures versus the year for both runs. Put time (generation) on the x-axis. Below the graph, write a paragraph that describes the relationship between time and population size.
2. What would your graph look like if there were more storks? Explain your thinking.
3. Answer the essential question: *How do births and deaths affect the size of a population?*

Data Table #1

Storks:2

Grim Reapers:2

Time per year:30 Seconds

Year	Living Paper Clip Creatures	Unconnected Paper Clips
0		
1		
2		
3		
4		
5		

Data Table #2

Storks:

Grim Reapers:

Time per year:

Year	Living Paper Clip Creatures	Unconnected Paper Clips
0		
1		
2		
3		
4		
5		

Birth Rate and Death Rate

Essential Question: *What factors might lead to high birth rates in certain regions of Canada? What factors might lead to low birth rates?*

Overview

Population growth is determined by four factors; birth rate, death rate, immigration, and emigration. Birth rate is determined by the number of live births that occur for every 1000 people in a given area. So, a birth rate of 15 means that for every 1000 people in that area, 15 new babies were born that year. A death rate is the number of deaths for every 1000 people in that area. So, a death rate of 8 means that for every 1000 people in a given area, eight people died that year. Immigration and emigration are the result of people moving in and out of a given area, such as a town or city. Immigration is the number of people that have moved into the given area within the year. Emigration is the number of people who have moved out of the given area within the year. When determining local populations such as cities and towns, all four factors are considered. When determining global population growth, only birth and death rates are the only factors.

In this activity, you will practice applying the idea of birth rate and death rate to actual populations. You can use these rates to determine whether a population is growing or shrinking. If the birth rate is higher than death rate, the population is growing. If the death rate is higher than birth rate, the population is shrinking. Birth and death rates are affected by many factors in a population. They include: clean living conditions, pre-natal education, health care for women and children, attitudes that the population has towards large families, and the number of young people in the area.

Analysis Questions

Use the charts on the following page to answer the questions below.

1. Is the birth rate in Canada increasing, decreasing, or staying the same? Justify your answer.
2. Which Canadian province had the highest death rate in 1999-2000?
3. The population of Nova Scotia in 1996 was 843,750 people. Use this number to calculate how many births occurred in Nova Scotia in 1996.
4. According to these data, which territory population most likely increased the most? How do you know?
5. What factors besides births and deaths could affect the overall population of this territory?
6. Answer the essential question: *What factors might lead to high birth rates in certain regions of Canada? What factors might lead to low birth rates?*

Death rate per 1,000 population[1]

	1995-1996	1996-1997	1997-1998	1998-1999	1999-2000
Canada	7.1	7.3	7.2	7.3	7.5
Newfoundland	7.0	7.5	7.9	7.9	8.5
Prince Edward Island	8.8	8.7	8.1	8.7	9.1
Nova Scotia	8.3	9.6	8.6	9.2	9.4
New Brunswick	7.8	8.1	8.2	8.6	9.0
Quebec	7.2	7.4	7.4	7.4	7.1
Ontario	7.0	7.2	7.1	7.2	7.4
Manitoba	8.4	8.5	8.4	8.8	9.0
Saskatchewan	8.3	8.7	8.7	8.7	9.1
Alberta	5.8	5.9	5.9	5.9	6.1
British Columbia	7.0	7.0	7.0	7.1	7.5
Yukon	4.6	4.0	4.1	5.0	5.3
Northwest Territories	3.6	4.3	3.6	4.52	3.8
Nunavut	x	4.2	3.3	4.12	5.2

x Data unavailable, not applicable or confidential.

1. From July 1 of one year to June 30 of the next year.

Birth rate per 1,000 population[1]

	1995-1996	1996-1997	1997-1998	1998-1999	1999-2000
Canada	12.6	12.0	11.5	11.2	10.9
Newfoundland	10.4	9.9	9.6	8.9	8.8
Prince Edward Island	13.2	11.8	11.1	10.9	10.7
Nova Scotia	11.6	10.9	10.5	10.0	9.9
New Brunswick	11.1	10.7	10.6	10.3	10.1
Quebec	11.9	11.4	10.6	10.1	10.0
Ontario	13.0	12.2	11.8	11.4	11.1
Manitoba	13.9	13.2	12.7	12.8	12.4
Saskatchewan	13.2	12.8	12.4	12.6	12.3
Alberta	13.9	13.3	13.0	13.0	12.7
British Columbia	12.2	11.6	11.0	10.7	10.3
Yukon	14.6	14.6	13.3	13.1	11.9
Northwest Territories	24.8	22.9	22.4	22.42	18.2
Nunavut	x	22.0	22.6	22.62	28.5

x Data unavailable, not applicable or confidential.

1. From July 1 of one year to June 30 of the next year.

Lesson 4
Is There a Limit?

Driving Question: *Are there any factors that limit population growth? Should we be concerned about them?*

Overview

The last lesson dealt with human population growth and the methods used to predict and calculate population changes. Population pyramids and birth/death rates make calculations and predictions easier. Why is it important to know how quickly or slowly a population is growing? Is there any reason to be concerned?

In this lesson, you will study examples from the animal world of population growth and its effects. You will finish recording data on your *Daphnia.* You will also read a story about a population of reindeer on an island near Alaska. Then you will take the ideas you've learned about population in this chapter and apply them to your own life.

Important Content

- Populations are dependent on resources to survive.
- Unchecked growth can lead to an imbalance between a population and the resources that support it.
- The size of the population that an area can support is called "carrying capacity".
- Personal decisions can change the resources we use.

Reindeer on St. Matthew Island

Essential Question: *What are the factors that affect the size of a population?*

Overview

As you look more closely at land and the organisms that live on it, you will notice how interdependent life is. Resources like food and energy are limited and many organisms are in competition for these resources. In this activity, you will examine factors that affect the size of a population.

Procedure

Read the attached article about a reindeer population on St. Matthew Island. When finished, answer the analysis questions.

Carrying Capacity and The Reindeer of St. Matthew Island

St. Matthew Island is located in the Bering Sea off the western coast of Alaska. It is 128 square miles of low-growing tundra grasses, with a few dwarf willow trees. High winds and fog are common and can occur at any time of year. The sub-Arctic island gets between 10 and 17 inches of rain and snow each year. Many years ago, the U.S. Coast Guard maintained a station on the island. That station was abandoned in 1944, leaving the island to its resident arctic foxes, singing voles, and a wide variety of sea birds.

Figure 1: Location of St. Matthew Island

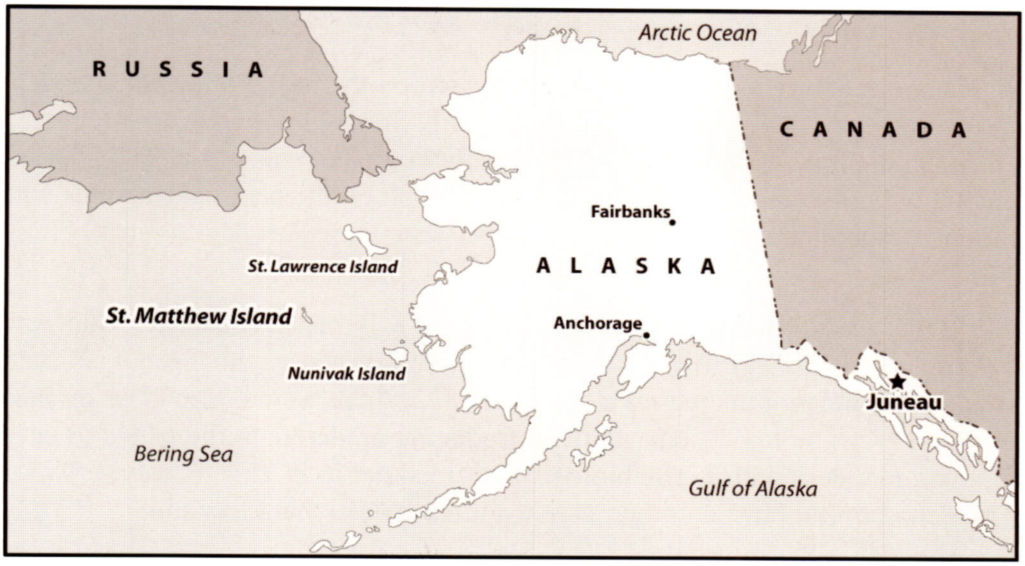

In 1944, wildlife biologists decided that the island could support a population of reindeer that was well adapted to the island's vegetation and climate. Reindeer were not native to the island and had never lived there. The biologists still believed that if the species was brought to the island to live, they would thrive. In 1944, 24 reindeer were introduced onto St. Matthew Island. The biologists believed that the *carrying capacity* of the island could easily support a stable population of 1600-2300 reindeer.

Figure 2: Reindeer grazing

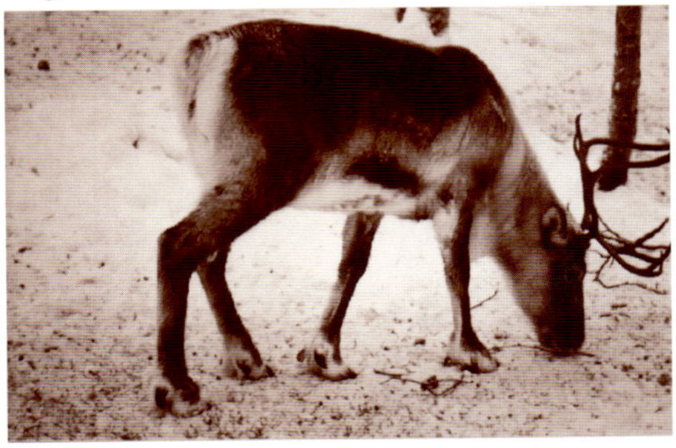

Carrying capacity is the number of individuals in a population that can be supported in a given area within natural resource limits, without degrading the natural environment for present and future generations. There are many factors that must be considered when determining carrying capacity for a population. These factors include: the abundance of food and water, the availability of shelter, the availability of areas for giving birth to young, and the presence and kind of predators. Predators are animals that hunt and eat other animals, thus controlling their population. Carrying capacity also considers the presence of other animals that might compete with a particular species for available resources.

Reindeer Are Introduced to St. Matthew Island

At first, the new reindeer thrived on St. Matthew Island. High-quality food was plentiful. There were no predators that hunted them. By 1957, the reindeer population had climbed to 1350 animals. The animals were healthy with an average body weight 24% higher than mainland reindeer.

By 1963, the lack of controls on the reindeer population on the island allowed their population to rise to 6000. Between 1963 and 1966, the continually growing population of reindeer exhausted the island's food resources. Nearly all of them died of starvation. The population crashed, leaving only 42 reindeer alive by 1966. The graph on the next page reveals what happened to the reindeer population on the island between their introduction in 1944 and their crash in 1966.

With so few reindeer left alive, the island's vegetation slowly began to recover. Sub-Arctic plants usually take much longer to grow than vegetation in warmer climates. Over several years, the reindeer population increased slowly. By 1975, there were 68 reindeer on the island. As the population grew, biologists considered introducing predators to the island to keep the reindeer population under control. The biologists decided not to do this, however. They feared the effects predators might have on other, native animal species on the island.

Graph 1: Population of reindeer on St. Matthew Island from 1944-1966

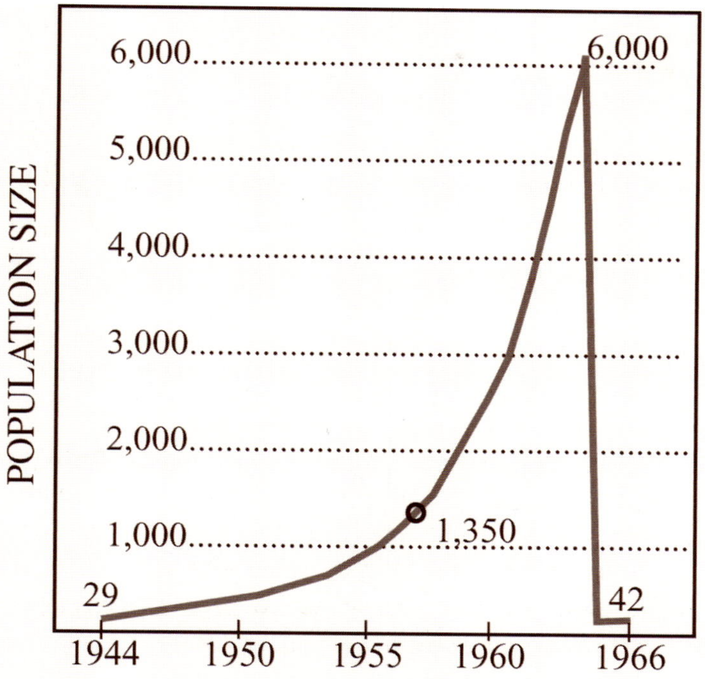

Assumed population of the St. Matthew Island reindeer herd. Actual counts are indicated on the population curve.

Analysis Questions

1. What are two factors in the rapid increase of the reindeer population on St. Matthew Island?
2. What are the factors that account for the reindeer population crash?
3. Some native animals on the island feed on plants and some birds use the island vegetation to build their nests. What can you infer about the likely impact of the reindeer on these other species?
4. What effects did the biologists fear might occur from introducing predators of reindeer to the island? Do you think their fear was justified? Why or why not?
5. Based on what you read in the text, define "*carrying capacity*?"
6. Did the reindeer population exceed the carrying capacity of the island? Use evidence to support your answer.
7. What would you predict might happen to the reindeer population after 1975? Explain your answer.
8. Answer the essential question: *What are the factors that affect the size of a population?*

Populations in Closed Systems

Essential Question: *Can we expect human populations to behave the same way other populations in closed systems behave?*

Materials

- data from your *Daphnia* observations. *(*Lesson 1: *Daphnia)*
- answers to analysis questions from Lesson 4: *Reindeer on St. Matthew Island*

Discussion Questions

1. In the *Daphnia* lab, we said that the *Daphnia* lived in a closed system. What do you think that meant?

2. It was also mentioned that the reindeer on St. Matthew Island were in a closed system. Do you agree?

3. Do you think the population of the United States is a closed system? Why or why not?

4. Is Earth a closed system? How might this affect the human population?

5. What happened to your *Daphnia* population during the two weeks of your study? Was it similar to or different from what happened to the reindeer? Was it similar to or different from what happened on the video about human populations? Was it similar to or different from what happened in the paper clip creatures game? What can you conclude about the relationship between birth/death rates and population change?

6. Why did the reindeer on St. Matthew Island die off? Why do you think your *Daphnia* population changed the way it did?

7. In at least three situations in this chapter, you have seen populations shrink rapidly. The situations were: disease like Black Death for humans, lack of food for the reindeer, and increased death rate as with the paper clip creatures. What methods do humans use (that animals cannot use) to prevent populations from shrinking this way? What do humans do to prevent their population from shrinking?

8. Answer the essential question: *Can we expect human populations to behave the same way other populations in closed systems behave?*

Personal Decisions

***Essential Question:** Based on your knowledge of growing populations, how many children will you choose to have?*

Overview

This chapter has covered many different topics about growing human populations. You have learned that birth rates and death rates are the measures of how many people are born and die in an area. Birth and death rates are used to determine if a population is growing. You have learned that the population of humans on Earth is growing rapidly. You have learned that people use resources, such as food and water, and that more people will use more resources. All of these effects are based on decisions that people make. People choose whether and when to have children. These decisions have a lot to do with cultural practices, economic constraints, and personal preferences. Our decisions affect not only ourselves but also the world community and the environment. We can understand the effects of our decisions by being better informed.

When we make decisions quickly, we are often influenced by things we might not be aware of. When you made your decision about how many children you will have, you might have been influenced by a number of different things. Being influenced is not a bad thing. It is important, however, to recognize where the influence is coming from. Then you can decide why you might or might not pay attention to that influence. Some influences include:

- Representative: I decided on this because it is similar to an experience I have had personally.
- Anchoring: The most recent thing I heard about was this, so I decided based on it.
- Availability: I will decide based on something that I understand rather than learning about something new.
- Framing: The information is presented to me in a way that makes this decision seem like the best one.

Class Discussion Questions

1. As a class, discuss your reasons for the decision you made.
2. Do any of your reasons look like the influences listed above?
3. Who else besides you will be affected by your decision to have many or few children? Did you consider these others when you made the decision?

Later in this chapter, you will learn a procedure for making decisions that will balance all of these factors.

Sample Decision

Essential Question: *How did this process help Anna make her decision?*

Overview

Making decisions is a big part of life and a big part of managing the environment in which we live. Politicians, company presidents and everyday citizens are constantly deciding how our resources should be managed. What is the best way to make these complicated decisions?

In Lesson 4: *Personal Decisions,* you made a decision that affects your own life and the environment you live in. In this activity, you will see an example of how Anna made that same decision. Anna used the **Environmental Decision Making Process**. You will learn to use this process and apply it to decisions you make throughout the year. Today, you will look through Anna's decision and see how the method is used. In a few weeks, you'll learn how to use it yourself.

Procedure

1. Look through the constraint and consideration lists, the consequence diagrams, the stakeholder charts, and the decision statements that Anna made.
2. Answer the analysis questions.

Analysis Questions

1. In the last activity, you read about different influences on decision making. Do you see any of those influences in Anna's decision?
2. If you had to write your own list of constraints and considerations for making this decision, what would be on each list?
3. Did Anna consider more stakeholders than you did when you made the same decision? Do you think this is good or bad?
4. Answer the essential question: *How did this process help Anna make her decision?*

Anna's Constraints and Considerations

Constraints are absolute requirements – things that the decision must not violate.

Considerations are things that would be nice to have but are not absolutely necessary.

Constraints:

1. I'll only have as many children as I can afford.
2. I think population growth is a problem, so I want to minimize population growth.
3. I definitely want at least one child.

Considerations:

1. I enjoyed having siblings when I was growing up, so I would like my kids to have brothers or sisters.
2. It would be nice to have a boy to carry on the family name.

Possible Choices:

1. Have only one child.
2. Have two children.
3. Have three children.

Anna's Consequence Diagrams

Consequence diagrams are a brainstorming tool to help you see the chain of events that will happen if you make that decision.

Figure 1: Consequence diagram for option #1, having only 1 child

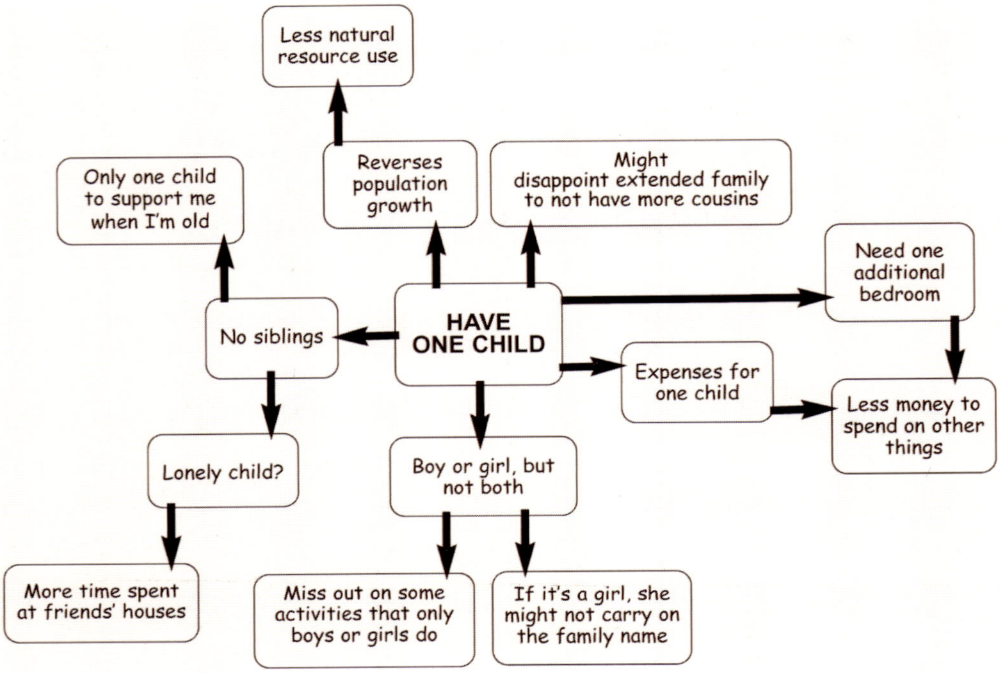

Figure 2: Consequence diagram for option #2, having 2 children

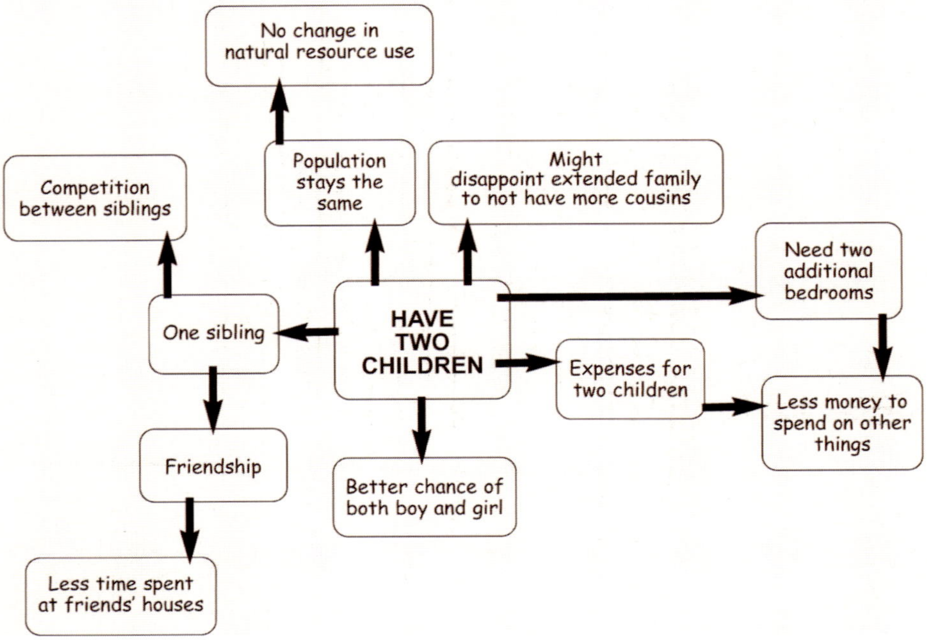

Figure 3: Consequence diagram for option #3, having 3 children

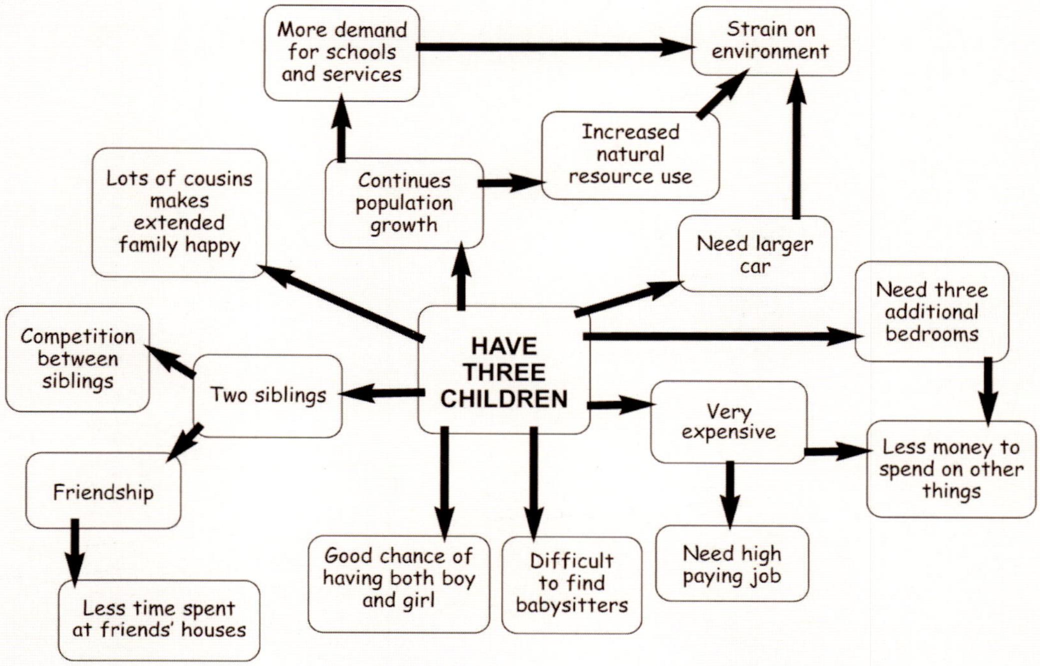

Anna's Stakeholder Charts

Stakeholder charts are organized to help you see who will be affected by the decision, how they will be affected and if negative effects are offset by greater good somewhere else.

Data Table 1: Stakeholder chart for option #1, having one child

Who are the stakeholders that will be affected by this action?	In what way(s) will they be affected?	+ or –	Is this effect the intended goal of the action or is it a side effect?	Has the stakeholder placed themselves in this position voluntarily and with appropriate understanding of the risks involved?	How important to YOU are the interests of this stakeholder? 1= very important 2= somewhat important 3= unimportant	If the effect is negative, do YOU feel it is directly offset by greater good elsewhere?
Me	Risks of pregnancy	-	Side effect	Yes	1	Yes
Both me and my husband	$$	-	Side effect	Yes	1	Yes
	Happiness in having a child	+	Goal			
Child	More attention from parents	+	Side effect	No	1	
	Possibly lonely	-	Side effect	No	1	Yes
Extended Family	Only one child to care for in an emergency	+	Side effect	No	2	
	Fewer grandchildren / cousins	-	Side effect			No
World Community and Environment	Slower population growth	+	Goal	No	2	
	Less resource use	+	Goal			

Data Table 2: Stakeholder chart for option #2, having 2 children

Who are the stakeholders that will be affected by this action?	In what way(s) will they be affected?	+ or –	Is this effect the intended goal of the action or is it a side effect?	Has the stakeholder placed themselves in this position voluntarily and with appropriate understanding of the risks involved?	How important to YOU are the interests of this stakeholder? 1= very important 2= somewhat important 3= unimportant	If the effect is negative, do YOU feel it is directly offset by greater good elsewhere?
Me	Risks of two pregnancies	-	Side effect	Yes	1	Yes
Both me and my husband	$$	-	Side effect	Yes	1	Yes
	Happiness in having two children	+	Goal			
Children	Less attention from parents	-	Side effect	No	1	Yes
	Sibling to love or hate	+ or -	Goal			
Extended Family	Two children to care for in an emergency	-	Side effect	No	2	Yes
	Two grandchildren / cousins	+	Side effect			
World Community and Environment	Maintain population growth	Neutral	Goal	No	2	
	Maintain resource use	Neutral	Goal			

Data Table 3: Stakeholder chart for option #3, having 3 children

Who are the stakeholders that will be affected by this action?	In what way(s) will they be affected?	+ or –	Is this effect the intended goal of the action or is it a side effect?	Has the stakeholder placed themselves in this position voluntarily and with appropriate understanding of the risks involved?	How important to YOU are the interests of this stakeholder? 1= very important 2= somewhat important 3= unimportant	If the effect is negative, do YOU feel it is directly offset by greater good elsewhere?
Me	Risks of 3 pregnancies	-	Side effect	Yes	1	Yes
Both me and my husband	$$	-	Side effect	Yes	1	Yes
	Happiness in having 3 children	+	Goal			
Children	Less attention from parents	-	Side effect	No	1	Yes
	Sibling to love or hate	+ or -	Goal			
Extended Family	Three children to care for in an emergency	-	Side effect	No	2	Yes
	Three grandchildren / cousins	+	Side effect			
World Community and Environment	Increase population growth	-	Side effect	No	2	No
	Increase resource use	-	Side effect			No

Anna's Decision Statement

A decision statement clearly states what the final decision is, and explains the decision, using both scientific evidence and information about personal values.

I have decided that I will have two children. This decision will meet all my criteria and should meet my considerations as well.

Criteria #1: I'll only have as many children as I can afford.

Having two children is more affordable than three. It is more expensive than one child, but I think I'll be able to afford it.

Criteria #2: I think population growth is a problem, so I want to minimize population growth.

By having two children, my husband and I will only be replacing ourselves. Thus, the population won't grow because of our actions. This will result in demand for resources staying the same.

Criteria #3: I definitely want at least one child.

Having two children meets this criterion.

Consideration #1: I enjoyed having brothers and sisters when I was growing up. So I would like my kids to have brothers or sisters.

Having two children meets this consideration. My kids will have one sibling to grow up with. I think this is important for a strong family. I might prefer to have more children so they have more brothers and sisters to grow up with. Having two children at least gives them some experience with this.

Consideration #2: It would be nice to have a boy to carry on the family name.

Having two children doesn't guarantee that one will be a boy, but it's a pretty good chance.

I made my decision by balancing the needs of the environment with my desire to have more than one child. The compromise was to have two children, so they have one brother or sister to grow up with. At the same time, two children will not increase the rate of population growth. If every couple has only two children, the population will eventually stabilize and stop growing.

CHAPTER 3

Resources

Chapter 3
Resources

Connections

In the last chapter, you saw why a Florida community needs a new school. Populations on Earth are growing quickly. This creates needs for more schools, more roads, more food, and more space to live. How can all these needs be met? Is there enough space on the planet for an unlimited growth of the human population? If the human population continues to grow, will it use up all of its available resources such as water, energy, and land?

Earth's resources are a growing concern for many. Government officials and environmental scientists are especially concerned about the consumption of energy and water. As you will see in Unit 2, running the air conditioner in the summer and the heating system in the winter creates a constant need for energy. Unit 3 will focus on one part of the U.S. where water resources are a critical issue. Cities and towns are facing the reality of dwindling water supplies and looking into new sources of fresh water. This chapter will introduce you to these resource issues.

So far, Unit 1 has focused on human populations and the use of resources. In later chapters, you will explore how humans share resources with plants and animals in ecosystems. Our consumption of resources affects our ability to meet our own needs and our impact on the natural environment.

In this chapter:

This chapter focuses on the resources that growing populations consume. You will focus on three resources: land, energy, and water. You will look at the availability of the resources that people need and find their locations on Earth. Throughout these explorations, keep in mind the places where people live and consider how resources are moved to meet people's needs. During your focus on land resources, you will calculate the amount of land needed to build a new school in Florida. At the end of this chapter, you will use the Environmental Decision Making Process to make a decision about changing your own resource consumption.

When you're done you'll be able to:

- Identify the resources you need to survive and determine ways to use your resources more efficiently.
- Label different regions of the Earth as resource rich or poor in energy, water, and land.
- Calculate the land area needed to build the new high school in Florida.
- Make a balanced environmental decision, using scientific evidence, social limits, and personal preferences.

Lesson 1
Land

Driving Question: *How much land is available on Earth? Is it enough to meet human needs?*

Overview

In the case of the Florida school you have read about, the major conflict is about land. The school needs space to house new students. But, the animals in the environment also need the land to survive. How can we find a balance? In this lesson, you will explore human land use and see how much land is required to support one person. You will start by calculating the land needed to build the school. You will also look at all the land resources you require to live your life. By the end of the lesson, you will compare that usage to the rest of the world. Most important, you will compare both these numbers to the actual amount of land available. This will give you an idea of whether we can continue to use land at the current rate. If not, we must adjust our usage or develop technology to make our land use more efficient.

Important Content

- The size of the population that an area can support is called carrying capacity.
- The average resource use and waste generated of an American is much larger than that of people from other countries. (This rate of use and waste is sometimes measured as an ecological footprint.)
- Energy, water, and land (especially arable land) are limited resources on Earth.

Area of a School

Essential Questions: *What is the minimum amount of space we need in order to build the school in Florida? What is the best amount of space to use for the school?*

Overview

The Florida school you have been asked to build has to support up to 2000 students. The school board has predicted this number based on the population growth for this area of Florida. What you do not know is how much land area this school needs to support those 2000 students. How much space per student does a school require? Today, you will answer this question. You will also consider which parts of a school are necessary and which are optional. Keep good notes on what you discuss because you will use them again when you make your final decision in Chapter 6.

Materials

For each group:

- 1 tape measure

Procedure

1. In a small group, brainstorm out all the different spaces needed for a school. Use the following questions to help you in your brainstorm:
   a. How many classrooms do you need for each subject area?
   b. Are all classrooms the same size?
   c. What other spaces are needed? (ex. lunchroom, gym, theater, etc…)

2. Narrow down your list to all the different places you think should be in a school.

3. Make a chart listing all the different types of spaces you think a school needs and how much area you think those spaces take up.

School Spaces	Estimated Area of this Space

4. Estimate how much space you think each of those places contains. To make your estimations, measure the length and the width of a corresponding room in your school with a tape measure.

   For example, if you are thinking about space for a science classroom, measure the length and width of your science classroom and multiply those two numbers. This will tell you the total area.

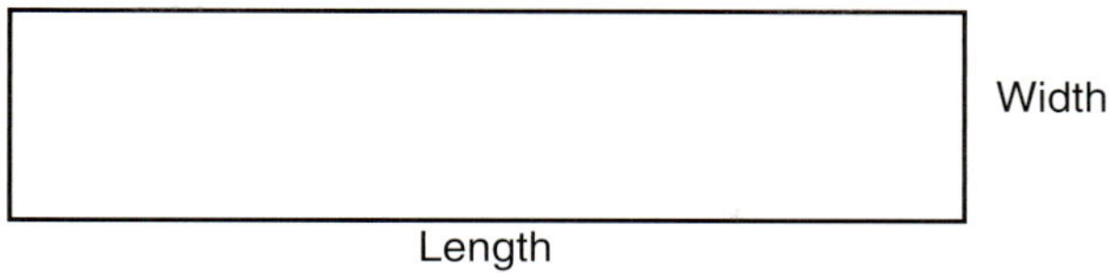

Length (ft) x Width (ft) = Total Area (square feet)

Make sure to make your measurements in square feet.

5. Discuss your estimates as a class. Did other students think of school spaces that you didn't consider?

6. Consider the area that you estimated for a certain use, like classrooms. Did you consider the number of classrooms as if all rooms would be used every period? Or did you estimate that some rooms would be empty at certain times of the day? How would that change your estimate of area needed?

7. As a class, determine the amount of space of a "generic school". What kinds of spaces will you have? Are they absolutely necessary? Complete the following chart as a class:

Space needed for	Estimated Area	Necessary? (yes, no, maybe)

8. Calculate the total area of the school buildings, parking, athletic areas, etc.

Analysis Questions

1. Did the estimated area of the school surprise you? Why?

2. Which parts of the school did you think were absolutely necessary? Which parts were optional? Did members of the class disagree on this?

3. When resources, including space, are used in a way that gets the most out of them, we say they are used efficiently. When resources are used in a way that is wasteful, we say they are inefficient. Are there ways of making the use of space in this school more efficient?

4. Answer the essential questions: *What is the minimum amount of space we need in order to build the school in Florida? What is the best amount of space to use for the school?* Consider the absolute minimum that would allow the school to run, and describe the best use of space. Include the features that would make the school better without being too inefficient.

Land Use Totals

Essential Question: *If everyone on the planet lived the way I do, how much land area would humans need?*

Overview

In the last activity, you considered how much space is required in a school for a growing population. But a school is only one of the things that a community needs. The next few lessons focus on the other resources required when the population grows in communities like the one in Florida that needs a new school. We will also look at how population growth in specific communities adds up to a growing global population.

When a population grows, they do not just need new schools. They also need homes, farms to grow food, roads, restaurants, shopping areas, and other services that take up land area. We know there is a limited amount of land available on the planet. So, it is important to measure the resources we use based on the amount of space they take up. In this lesson, we look at the land required to support one person. You. In the next lesson, we will look at the land required to support population growth at the level of countries and the entire world.

Materials

For each group:

- calculator

Procedure

The chart on the next page contains estimates of how much land is required to produce the materials to support common activities. For example, the land required to support diet is the land required to produce the food. The land required for home construction includes the land required to grow the lumber. The estimates are based on averages for Americans.

1. From the chart, select the categories (food, living space, roads, landfills, mining for consumable goods, clothing, etc) that apply to you.

2. Add up the land area that is necessary to support your lifestyle. You can subtract the numbers if you only use part of that resource. For example, if you and your brother share a car, you can cut the numbers for fuel consumption in half.

Data Table 1: Constructing your environmental impact

Activity	Land Area Needed for an Average American	Your Total
Diet (choose one): Vegetarian	0.0075 km^2 farmland	
Low meat consumption	0.009 km^2 farmland	
Average American meat consumption	0.0097 km^2 farm and pasture	
House construction	0.0043 km^2 forests	
Paper, packaging	0.0014 km^2 forest land	
Clothing	0.0015 km^2 forest and pasture	
Private living space	0.0008 km^2 urban land	
School and/or work space	*From* Lesson 1: *Area of a School*	
Shopping, restaurants and services	0.0002 km^2 urban land	
Roads and highways	0.0010 km^2 urban land	
Energy for one car	0.0060 km^2 forest land	
Energy for public transportation	0.0007 km^2 forest land	
Energy for transport and manufacture of goods	0.0167 km^2 forest land	

Notes on the table: 1 m^2 = 0.000001 km^2

There is no one person that can be categorized as an average American. The land area values for the activities represent a national average.

These calculations convert energy use into an amount of land by estimating the amount of forest land necessary to remove carbon dioxide from the air. When fossil fuels (oil, gasoline, coal, natural gas) are burned to make electricity or to drive a car, oxygen is converted into carbon dioxide, which is released into the air. Plants (especially trees) convert that carbon dioxide back into oxygen, which we breathe. So, the numbers in the chart show the amount of land that is required to convert the carbon dioxide back into oxygen.

Analysis Questions

1. What do you think the land that is required to produce clothing is used for?

2. What activities do you do that require paper? Name some of the forms of packaging that you come in contact with every day? What is that packaging made of?

3. What is the total land area required to support you?

4. If you were required to reduce this to 0.0400 km^2, what would you be willing to give up? What if you had to reduce it to 0.0350 km^2?

5. Do you participate in activities that are not in the chart that require land? Estimate their land use.

6. These calculations do not include water use. Think about how you might measure water use as land area. Write a paragraph explaining how you think it could be done.

7. Answer the essential question: *If everyone on the planet lived the way I do, how much land area would humans need?* Use the total land area you calculated for yourself, the population of the Earth as six billion (6,000,000,000), and the total land area (not including oceans) of the planet as 150,000,000 km^2.

Sustainability and Ecological Footprints

Essential Questions: *How does the amount of space I need compare with that of other people on Earth? What impact does that have on where my resources come from?*

Read the following article and answer the questions that follow.

Reading

As you have already seen, the growing population in Florida is part of a global trend of population growth. In this reading, we consider the demand for land required by growing populations at the country and world level and examine the variation in land requirements of people in different countries.

Sustainability

An important question to consider when looking at our use of natural resources is: *Is our use of resources sustainable*? Resource use is sustainable when it can be continued into the future indefinitely. Resource use is unsustainable if there is a limit to how long we can continue to use resources in that way.

Whether or not the use of a particular resource is sustainable depends on the nature of the resource and how it is used. For example, human use of oil as a fuel is not sustainable because there is a limited supply of oil on Earth, and the way we use it (burning it) makes it unavailable for future use. Scientists understand that one day humans will use up all of Earth's available oil, and that we will need to identify other sources of energy that people will use instead of oil in the future. In contrast, metals like iron are also a limited resource on Earth, but the way we use iron does not destroy it. Iron can be re-used. So, the sustainability of our use of iron depends on how much of it we need at one time and how efficiently we recycle it. Land, the topic of this reading, is limited, but it can be re-used indefinitely under proper circumstances. For example, land that is used to grow crops for food can be re-used year after year if careful practices are used to preserve the fertility of the land.

Ecological Footprint Analysis

Scientists who try to understand whether human activities are sustainable have developed a way of determining the sustainability of resource use that they call *ecological footprint analysis.* The calculation that you made in the previous lesson was an analysis of your ecological footprint. The idea of a footprint is that if someone were to put together all the land necessary to support one person's activities in one place, that land would represent his or her "footprint." In fact, the land that makes up an individual's ecological footprint can be located anywhere in the world because people rely on resources from many places to support their activities.

The word "ecological" appears in the name because an ecological footprint is a measurement of the *ecologically productive* land that a person's lifestyle requires. Ecologically productive land is land that is fertile enough to support forests, agriculture, and/or animal life. The total amount of ecologically productive land in a location is called its "biological capacity." Therefore, each country has its own biological capacity and the world has a biological capacity.

When you combine the ecological footprints of all the people in a country or the world, you have a measure of the human demand for resources. This number can be compared to the biological capacity in that country or the world. When human demands exceed biological capacity, there are not enough resources to support that population. If a country's demand is greater than its capacity, then it can obtain resources from other countries. However, if global demand exceeds capacity, then humans are using resources more quickly than they are being replaced. This situation is called "overshoot," or, an ecological deficit. If an ecological deficit continues for too long, then there will no longer be enough resources to support the population.

The concept of an ecological footprint is very helpful for considering the sustainability of human resource use. However, different scientists have developed different ways of calculating ecological footprints, and there are disagreements about how fair and accurate these ecological footprint analyses are. Some people argue that they underestimate the actual resource requirements and others argue that they overestimate.

One organization that has developed methods for calculating ecological footprints is Redefining Progress. Redefining Progress is a non-profit organization in the United States whose mission is to "shift the economy and public policy toward sustainability." They have worked with scientists to develop a way of calculating ecological footprints. They have calculated ecological footprints for the world and for different countries using data from the United Nations.

According to Redefining Progress, the average world citizen has an ecological footprint of 0.022 km^2 (5.4 acres). The average German's footprint is 0.043 km^2 (10.6 acres) and the average American's is 0.096 km^2 (23.7 acres). You can examine the figures for many countries in the table on the following pages. In many countries, the demand for ecological capacity exceeds its available ecologically productive area. These countries are running an ecological deficit.

According to Redefining Progress's calculations, there are 0.019 km^2 (4.7 acres) of ecologically productive space available per person on Earth. Since they calculated that the world's average ecological footprint was 0.022 km^2 (5.4 acres) per person in 2000, they concluded that humanity was exceeding the biosphere's ecological capacity by over 15 percent. Another organization, the Global Footprint Network, reported similar results using their own ecological footprint analysis in 2004.

Ecological Footprint Analysis and Sustainability

Land is a limited resource, and ecologically productive land is even more limited. In order for our use of ecologically productive land to be sustainable, human society must be able to obtain all the resources that we need at any time from that land, and we must use that land in a way that it continues to be ecologically productive to support the needs of future generations.

At the 1992 United Nations Earth Summit in Brazil, the governments of the world committed themselves to the goal of sustainability. The idea of ecological footprints was developed to help measure sustainability. By comparing the ecological footprint of all the people in the world to the amount of ecologically productive land on Earth, we can determine whether our global consumption of resources is sustainable.

Analysis Questions

1. What does "ecologically productive" mean?
2. According to Redefining Progress, what is the ecological footprint for an average world citizen?
3. If we divided the planet equally among all inhabitants, how much ecologically productive land would each person get?
4. Use the information in the table on the next page. List the countries whose people have the five largest and five smallest ecological footprints.
5. If a country has a surplus in the last column of the table (if the number appears in parentheses), then it has enough ecologically productive land to support its population's activities. Countries with a deficit in that column must import food and goods to support their population. List five countries with the largest surpluses. List five countries that are overshooting their biological capacity (in deficit).
6. Do you think the ecological footprint of people living in Florida is larger or smaller than the average for the United States? Why?
7. Redefining Progress's goal is to encourage the sustainable use of resources. Which would help them achieve their goal better, overestimating or underestimating ecological footprints? Why? If you wanted to judge if their estimates are accurate yourself, how might you do that?
8. Answer the essential questions: *How does the amount of space I need compare with that of other people on Earth? What impact does that have on where my resources come from?*

Data Table 1: Average Ecological Footprints of the World Calculated in 2000 (Source: Redefining Progress)

COUNTRY	Population (Millions in year 2000)	Ecological Footprint (km^2)	Current Capacity (km^2)	Deficit (surplus) (km^2 per capita)
Argentina	37.0	0.032	0.075	(0.043)
Australia	19.1	0.071	0.118	(0.047)
Austria	8.1	0.049	0.019	0.030
Bangladesh	137.4	0.005	0.004	0.001
Brazil	170.4	0.024	0.071	(0.048)
Canada	30.8	0.086	0.126	(0.040)
Chile	15.2	0.030	0.042	(0.012)
China	1,282.4	0.014	0.010	0.003
Denmark	5.3	0.053	0.035	0.018
Egypt	67.9	0.012	0.006	0.006
Finland	5.2	0.070	0.087	(0.017)
France	59.2	0.057	0.023	0.035
Germany	82.0	0.043	0.014	0.028
India	1,008.9	0.008	0.007	0.001
Indonesia	212.1	0.010	0.020	(0.010)
Italy	57.5	0.033	0.009	0.024
Japan	127.1	0.039	0.006	0.033
Korea, Rep.	46.7	0.024	0.008	0.016
Malaysia	22.2	0.030	0.037	(0.007)
Mexico	98.9	0.026	0.019	0.007
Netherlands	15.9	0.038	0.008	0.030
Norway	4.5	0.082	0.055	0.027
Pakistan	141.3	0.007	0.004	0.002
Philippines	75.7	0.011	0.007	0.005
Poland	10.0	0.034	0.017	0.017
Russia	145.5	0.043	0.053	(0.010)
South Africa	43.3	0.035	0.034	0.001
Spain	39.9	0.049	0.018	0.031
Sweden	8.8	0.079	0.072	0.007
Switzerland	7.2	0.053	0.014	0.039
Thailand	62.8	0.014	0.014	0.000
Turkey	66.7	0.022	0.014	0.008
United Kingdom	59.6	0.047	0.014	0.034
U.S.A.	283.2	0.096	0.046	0.050
WORLD AVERAGE	6,056.7	0.022	0.019	0.003

Deficit is calculated by subtracting Ecological Footprint from Current Capacity.
(Numbers may not add up due to rounding.)

Arable Land

Essential Question: *Where is most of the world's farmland compared to where people who consume their products live?*

Read the following article and use the map that follows to answer the analysis questions.

Reading

In *Sustainability and Ecological Footprints*, you learned the definition of "ecologically productive land." In this activity, you will look at one specific type of land: arable land. Arable land is land that is suitable for growing crops. One concern for governments and environmental scientists is, do we have enough arable land to provide sufficient food for the growing human population on Earth? Even though the Earth has an enormous amount of land, only a small part of that land (9%) is arable, and not all of the arable land is being used for farming.

When arable land is being used to grow crops, we say that the land is being used for cultivation. In the U.S., nearly 470 million acres of arable land are currently being used for cultivation. Of these, more than 1 million acres are converted to other uses each year, such as housing, transportation, and industry. Another 2 million acres of cropland are lost to farming annually because of erosion (blowing or washing away of surface soil), salinization (accumulation of salt in the soil), and waterlogging (accumulation of water in the soil).

One reason so many people can live in one location is that their food can be transported to them from other places. Transporting large quantities of food over long distances is a relatively recent development in human history. Towns and cities used to be small enough that the nearby land could support their entire population, even in years of drought and small harvests. Because of the availability of inexpensive transportation and technology for preserving food, people no longer need to live close to the sources of their food. As a result, throughout the world, the populations of towns and cities have steadily increased.

Analysis Questions

1. Why is the total supply of arable land in the U.S. decreasing every year?

2. Look at the map on the next page. Where do you find little or no farmland? Why do you think these places have little farmland?

3. Compare the map of arable land on the next page with your map of population distribution from Chapter 2, Lesson 3: *Distribution of Humans.* How do the locations of where most people live compare to where arable land is located?

4. Answer the essential question: *Where is most of the world's farmland compared to where people who consume their products live?*

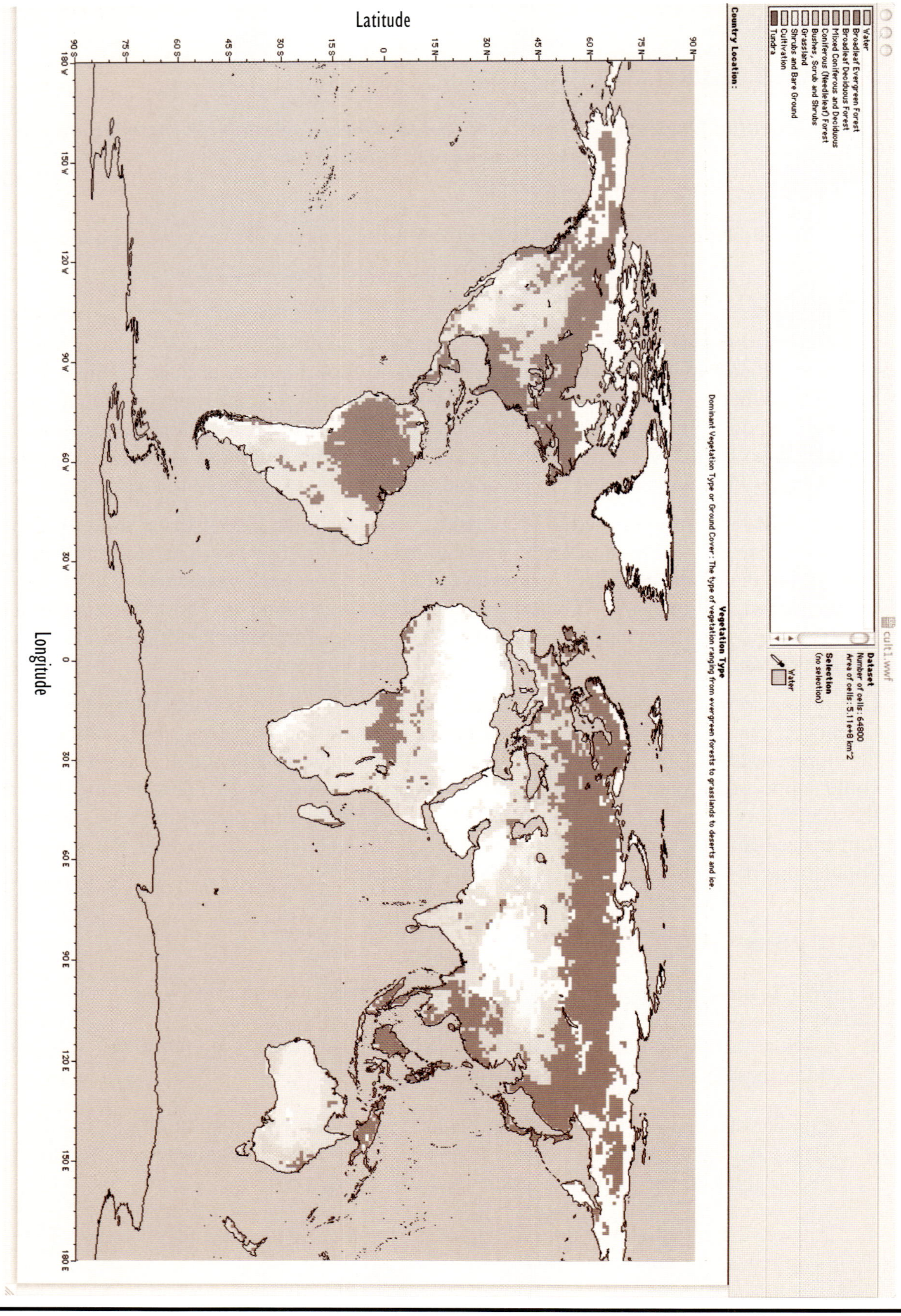

Figure 1: Ground cover information for the world

Carrying Capacity, Technology, and Decision Making

Essential Question: *Why don't we know if the Earth can continue to support the growing human population?*

Read the following passage and answer the analysis questions.

Reading

This lesson deals with the question of how many people the Earth can support. To really understand the question, you have to take a global perspective because a local or national perspective could be misleading. From a local perspective, if you have plenty of open space around you, you might conclude that there must be room to support more people. From a national perspective, if you see the U.S. export food to other countries you might conclude that we have more than enough food.

However, limits that are not obvious at the local or national level become clearer when considering the entire Earth. It is difficult to determine the carrying capacity of any local area because resources are transported over large distances. Technology enables us to stretch the human carrying capacity of local ecosystems. In the past, people were limited to living in locations that could provide them with all the resources that they needed. If they started to use more resources than the land could provide, they could see it in their local environment. Today, if people live where there is not enough arable land to grow crops, they can easily import food from other areas. If they live where there are no forests for wood, they bring wood from other areas. This importing and exporting makes it harder to see whether our population is growing too quickly for the land to support us.

To understand how many people our planet can support, we have to look at the entire Earth as a system. There are two important variables in determining human needs for resources: consumption and technology.

As you have learned, consumption of resources per person varies widely around the world. In general, wealthier societies have higher rates of consumption per person than poorer societies.

At present, both the human population and the average consumption of resources per person are increasing. At the same time, the productive land and other natural resources that are available to support humans are fixed.

As you learned in the previous chapter, carrying capacity is the maximum population of a species that can be supported in a habitat without causing a decrease in the productivity of that habitat. However, humans have the ability to increase the carrying capacity of the land through technology and through changes in lifestyle.

Technology can increase the quantity of resources we can obtain from the Earth and how much use we get out of those resources. For example, new mining technologies now enable energy companies to obtain oil and natural gas from locations that were inaccessible even a decade ago. Technology can also increase the efficiency of our use of resources. When we increase the efficiency with which we use a resource, we can do more with the same quantity of that resource. For example, since the 1970s, automotive engineers have developed technologies that allow cars to drive more miles with the same amount of fuel. Over a period of centuries, farmers and agricultural scientists have developed more efficient farming techniques that allow farmers to grow crops that produce more food in the same amount of land.

Humans also can increase the carrying capacity of Earth by making decisions about how to use the available resources. Individuals and communities can choose to change their lifestyles in a number of ways, so that they consume fewer resources. Of course, they can also make different choices that would increase their need for resources. In an upcoming lesson, you will get a chance to consider a decision about your lifestyle that has implications for the resources required to support you. You will consider different options for what foods to eat.

Experts disagree on what is the carrying capacity of Earth. Some argue that there are definite biological limits to Earth's carrying capacity. They are concerned that the growing human population is at risk of reaching or exceeding those limits. Others insist that we will continue to develop technologies and make decisions that will enable us to meet the needs of the growing global population with the available natural resources. This is an important debate.

Some experts in the past predicted that even the size of the human population that we have today would exceed the limits of Earth's carrying capacity. They were wrong. We are currently able to meet the needs of today's population. However, we still have two important questions that can only be answered with time:

- Is our current use of Earth's resources sustainable?
- Can Earth's resources support our population as it continues to grow?

Analysis Questions

1. Why do we need to consider the entire Earth when we talk about available land and carrying capacity? Why can't we just consider the U.S., or even our home state?

2. How might technology increase Earth's carrying capacity for humans?

3. Answer the essential question: *Why don't we know if the Earth can continue to support a growing human population?*

Lesson 2
Energy

Driving Question: *Where is energy available on Earth, and how is the demand for energy changing?*

Overview

In the last lesson, you learned about humans' needs for land resources. This lesson focuses on energy resources: their location, abundance, and usefulness. You will make predictions about the amount of energy available from the Sun on different parts of the Earth. You will test your predictions by using software called WorldWatcher to compare your predictions to the actual air temperatures on Earth. You will compare areas that have a lot of energy (in the form of warm temperatures) to areas where most people live. You will discuss the resource use associated with those patterns. You will also explore other types of energy and how much of it is available for human use.

The resources you studied in Lesson 1 are all necessary for human survival. You probably noticed that most of the limiting resources could be described as either limited water, limited energy, or limited food. In the next three lessons, you will look at each resource category in more detail starting with energy. You will determine how much of the resource is necessary to support yourself and where that resource comes from. Later in this unit, you will continue your study of land resources. Later in the year, Unit 2 will focus on energy resources, and Unit 3 will cover water resources.

Important Content

- We use energy for many reasons. We get it from many sources, including the Sun and fossil fuels.
- Energy, water and land (especially arable land) are limited resources on Earth.

Energy Resources

Essential Questions: *What energy resources do we need? Where are they available?*

Overview

Review the list of resources you developed in Lesson 1. Think more carefully about the energy resources that you use. Energy is not just electricity. Think of the energy your body uses, and the energy used to heat your home and move your car.

Answer the following questions with your class:

Class Discussion

1. Discuss the different types and uses of energy resources.

2. As a class, fill out the following chart:

Type	What it is used for	Where it comes from	Abundance on Earth

3. If you live somewhere that lacks a particular source of energy, can you substitute another energy source in its place? For example, if you live where there is little energy from the Sun but lots of coal, can you keep your house warm?

4. What could you do if you lived in a place that had neither source?

Energy from the Sun

Essential Question: *How do you think the energy from the Sun is distributed around the Earth?*

Overview

Why do you think so many people are choosing to live in Florida? One reason is the weather. Florida is warm year-round. What makes Florida warm? The energy from the Sun.

You discussed many different kinds of energy in the last activity. Today, you will focus on energy from the Sun. You will focus on sunlight because all forms of energy on Earth come from the Sun. For example, food production and farming are dependent on the Sun's energy to help plants grow. Even the energy in the fossil fuels (oil, natural gas, and coal) that we burn for heating, generating electricity, and running machinery originally came from the Sun. Fossil fuels are the remains of decomposed plants and animals that grew long ago using the Sun's energy.

In this activity and the next one, we will look at temperature as an indicator of how the energy from the Sun is distributed around the Earth. We will also compare the patterns of temperature to the patterns of where people live.

The temperature of a given location is largely determined by how much energy from the Sun that location has received recently. Therefore, it is a good indicator of the amount of energy that location receives from the Sun.

Your task in this activity is to draw a map showing what you think the temperature is around the world in July.

Materials

For each group:

- blank temperature map for each student.
- 6 colored crayons, pencils, or markers (purple, green, blue, yellow, orange, red)

Procedure

1. Discuss as a class what temperatures you think should correspond with each of the six colored crayons. Because you only have six colors to work with, each color will represent a range of temperatures. For example:

-50°F to -25°F	=	color #1
-24ºF to 0ºF	=	color #2
1°F to 32°F	=	color #3
33°F to 60°F	=	color #4
61ºF to 85ºF	=	color #5
86°F to 112°F	=	color #6

2. Color in the map showing what you think the average temperature is in each part of the world for the month of July. Color each location on the map with only one color.

   Be sure to color both the continents and the oceans, but base your colors on what you think the air temperatures are in those places, not the temperatures of the land or water.

   Do not worry if you are unsure. This activity is just a way to explore what your ideas about temperature are. Your maps will not be graded for accuracy in this activity! This should take you about 10 minutes.

Analysis Questions

1. How did you decide what temperatures to put where?
2. Where did you start and how did you proceed?
3. Which parts of the world did you feel certain about?
4. Which parts of the world did you feel uncertain about?
5. How did you fill in the parts that you were uncertain about?
6. What would you have done differently if you were doing a map for January? For April? For October?
7. What questions do you have about temperature that you did not have before you tried to create your own temperature map?

Temperatures on Earth

Essential Question: *In what locations on Earth do people depend more on sources of energy other than the Sun for food and warmth?*

Overview

In this activity, you will continue to explore the distribution of energy from the Sun around the world. People that live in places that receive less energy from the Sun must get more energy from other sources. They are more dependent on other energy resources.

In this activity, you will get a chance to look at actual temperatures on Earth and compare them to your ideas about temperatures on Earth that you drew on your maps in the previous activity.

To study temperatures on Earth, you will use computer software called WorldWatcher. The software will allow you to draw in your predicted temperatures. You will also see maps of actual temperatures and compare the two. You will use WorldWatcher throughout this course.

Materials

For each group:

- Your colored temperature maps from Lesson 2: *Energy from the Sun* used in Step 5
- WorldWatcher software

Procedure

1. Start WorldWatcher according to your teacher's instructions. The Welcome to WorldWatcher screen will help you navigate through many of WorldWatcher's features.

2. To access the WorldWatcher data and files, click on the Looking At The Environment button.

Figure 1: WorldWatcher welcome page

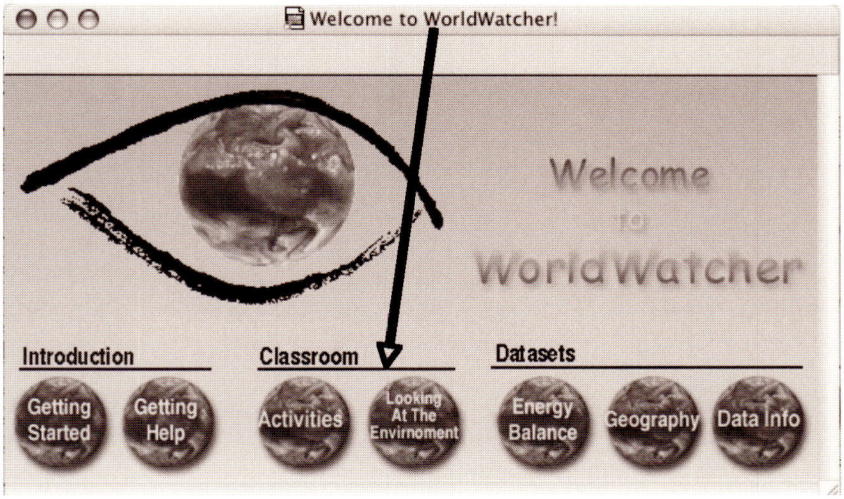

3. Click the icon next to Looking At The Environment (LATE) Project Resources. From this screen, you can select which unit and activity you need. Today, you are working on Lesson 2*: Temperatures on Earth.*

4. (From here until the end of the activity, these directions will follow the directions in the WorldWatcher notebook on your screen.) To get started, open the **Blank Temperature Map** by clicking on the appropriate icon in the notebook.

5. Use the Paintbrush, Rectangular Marquee, and Paintcan tools to color the temperature map in WorldWatcher. Use the same values you drew on your temperature map in the last activity (*Energy from the Sun).*

6. Select a color by clicking the Paintbrush tool and "dipping" the Paintbrush into the color scheme on the top of the map . The color you select will appear in the box on the far right side of the color scheme.

7. There are two ways you can paint the map. You can use either the Paintbrush or the Paintcan. To use the Paintbrush, place the brush over the square you want to paint and click. If you hold the mouse button, you can paint more than one cell at a time. To change temperatures, "dip" the brush into a different value.

8. If you want to paint many cells at once, select a group of cells using the Rectangular Marquee. After you have selected the cells you want to paint, click the Paintcan. Then "fill" it from the color scheme, and paint your selection.

9. If you need help using the paint tools, WorldWatcher has Help files in the Help menu at the top of the screen. For help using buttons in the toolbar, look for Help Section 4-Toolbars.

Comparing Your Prediction to Actual Temperatures

10. Click the icon in the notebook to view the **Actual Average July Temperature Map**.

11. Look at the new map next to the map you drew.

Stop and Think

Write down the differences between your predictions and the actual surface temperature.

12. Notice the information that is displayed just above the visualization. The arrow and the information below the color bar follow your mouse as you move it around.

13.  Select the Synchronize Mouse tool in the tool bar. As you move the mouse around in one window, you can see it moving in any other open windows.

Stop and Think

Pick four places around the world that you're interested in. Record the differences between your map and the actual temperature map for those locations.

14. Use the Zoom tools to zoom in on an image . (If you are using a Macintosh, you will have only one Zoom tool, which looks like this: . Hold the option key to zoom out.)

Using Selections to Compare Regions

15. Use the Rectangular Marquee tool  and the Lasso  to select regions in the visualizations. The information area at the top of the window shows the minimum, maximum, and mean (average) values for both the whole image and the area you've selected.

16. Use the Select by Underlay option in the Select menu to select a particular country, state, or province.

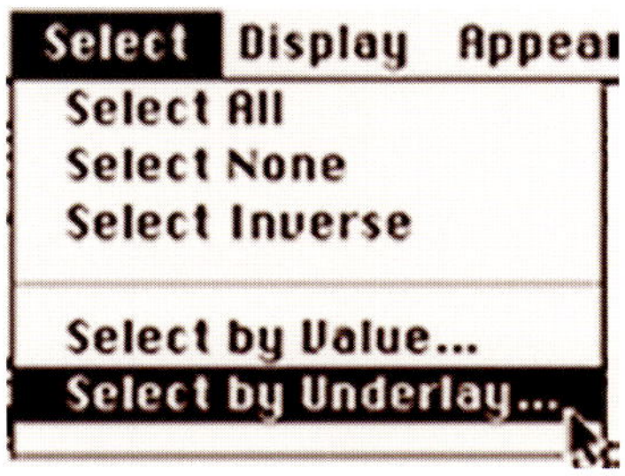

Stop and Think

Select four regions from around the world. Record the minimum, maximum, and mean values for those regions for both your map and the measured temperature for those regions.

Comparing Visualizations by Subtraction

17. To perform a subtraction, make sure that your July temperature is the top window. Select the Window Math Operation tool in the toolbar . Select Subtraction as the math operation. Select the average July temperature as Window B. Give this new window a descriptive title.

18. The new visualization should show:

    - areas where your temperatures are warmer as shades of red.
    - areas where your temperatures are cooler as shades of blue.
    - areas where both temperatures are very similar as white or light.
    - areas where both temperatures are very different as dark red or dark blue.

19. You can also use the Histogram function to compare the histograms of the two images. You may need to use the Zoom tools to zoom in on the histogram.

Stop and Think

Describe the areas where your estimated temperature was closest to the actual temperature. Describe those areas where your estimate was farthest off.

Analysis Questions

1. Record any new questions you have about temperature now that you've compared your map with the measured temperatures.

2. Think about the different types of energy covered in Lesson 2: *Energy Resources*. What type of energy did you explore with WorldWatcher today?

3. Compare the WorldWatcher visualization of average temperature to the map of population distribution in Chapter 2. Do most people live where it is warm or cold? Why?

4. In areas of the world that do not receive much warmth from the Sun, what might people do to keep warm? In areas of the world that get lots of warmth from the Sun, what might people do to keep cool? What types of energy do these activities use?

5. Energy from the Sun affects the crops that can be grown in a region. What do you expect to see in terms of food availability in areas with little solar energy? In areas with lots of solar energy?

6. Answer the essential question: *In what locations on Earth do people depend more for sources of energy other than the Sun for food and warmth?*

Skills Practice

Essential Question: *How can you use WorldWatcher to answer questions about a dataset?*

Overview

In this activity, you will learn WorldWatcher skills that you will use throughout the year. As you work through this lesson, answer the questions on the *Skills Practice Worksheet*. If you need help performing a task in WorldWatcher, use the Help menu on the top of the screen.

Materials

- WorldWatcher
- WorldWatcher Skills Practice Worksheet

Reading Data

1. From the Looking at the Environment Project Resources button, open Resources 2, showing surface temperature in January 1982. Answer Worksheet Question 1.

Getting Help

2. Open the WorldWatcher Glossary from the Help menu. Answer Worksheet Question 2.

3. Click the icon to go to the overlay help page. Answer Worksheet Question 3.

4. Answer Question 4.

Overlay

5. Switch the overlay on the January 1982 surface temperature dataset to Country Outlines. Answer Question 5.

Underlay

An underlay is similar to an overlay. Instead of lines laid over the dataset, an underlay contains text information *under* the dataset. The information contained in the underlay is displayed at the bottom of the Readout Panel.

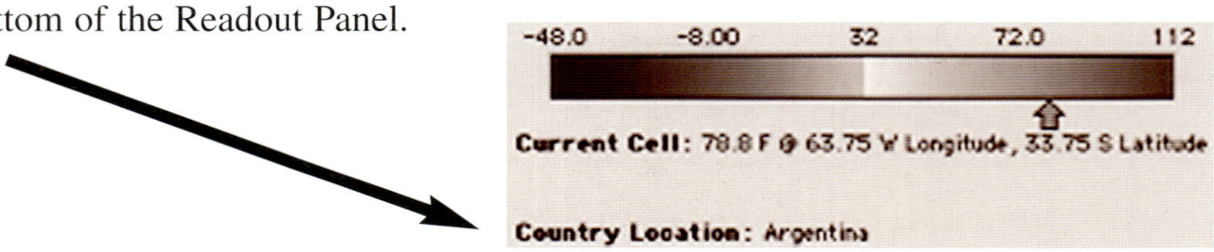

6. Go to the Display menu for the current dataset to change the Underlay settings. Answer Question 6.

7. Answer Question 7.

Selections

WorldWatcher allows you to select cells and gather information about your selections. There are several tools you can use to make selections.

- From the toolbar, you can choose the  Rectangle Marquee or the  Lasso Marquee.
- From the Select menu, you can Select By Value or Select By Underlay.

You learned to use the Rectangle Marquee and the Lasso Marquee in the last activity. Today, you will learn to use the options in the Select menu.

Select by Underlay

This feature allows you to select cells based on the information contained in the underlay. Choose Select By Underlay from the Select menu. Highlight the underlay value in the list you wish to select. (You can pick more than one value by pressing shift + click.) Click OK to make your selection.

8. Look at the January 1982 surface temperature dataset. Choose Select By Underlay from the Select menu. Highlight Iceland and click OK. Answer Question 8.

Select by Value

This feature allows you to select cells based on the value of that data in the cell. Choose Select By Value from the Select menu. You can select cells whose value is greater than a specific number, less than a specific number, or between two numbers.

9. Select all the places on Earth where the average temperature in January 1982 was greater than 78ºF. Answer Question 9.

Hide Unselected

Sometimes, like in Question 9, it is difficult to tell which areas are selected and which are not. To only display the cells which you have selected, choose Hide Unselected from the Display menu. This will hide the cells which are not selected. To return the display to normal, choose Show Unselected from the same menu.

10. Hide the unselected cells and answer Question 10.

Adding To / Subtracting From / Selecting From Within Current Selection

So far, you have created only new selections. If you already have a portion of a dataset selected, WorldWatcher allows you add cells to your selection by choosing Add to the current selection. You can remove cells from the selection by choosing Subtract from the current selection. In this window, you can also choose Select from within the current selection.

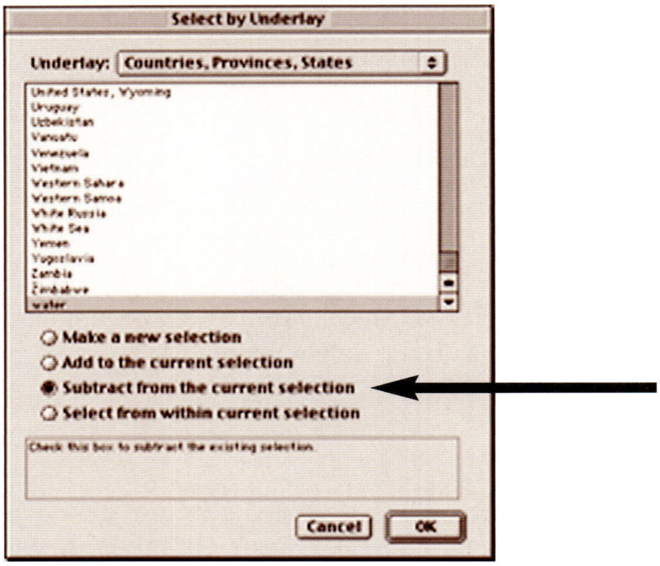

11. Working with the selection from Question 10, use Select by Underlay to subtract all of the cells that are water. Answer Question 11.

Selecting In Two Datasets
You have already worked with the Synchronize Mouse  feature. With this feature on, anything you do in one visualization window also happens to the other open windows. Moving your cursor above a cell will reveal the data value for that cell in all open visualizations. Zooming or making a selection will also happen in all open visualization windows.

12. Clear the selections from your dataset by choosing Select None from the Select menu. Open the dataset showing the average temperature in July 1982. Use Synchronize Mouse and the Rectangle Marquee to answer Question 12.

13. Make a new selection or selections using all the skills you have learned. Answer Questions 13 and 14.

WORLDWATCHER 2: SKILLS PRACTICE WORKSHEET

1. Complete the following table. Remember to include units in your answers!

Question	Answer
What color corresponds to 37° F?	
What is the maximum temperature in this dataset?	
What is the minimum temperature in this dataset?	
Chicago, Illinois is located at approximately 88.75° W longitude, 43.75° N latitude. What was the average temperature in Chicago in January 1982?	

2. Write the definition of overlay in the box below.

overlay:

3. What is the heading in large blue letters on the top of this page?

____

4. Fill in the blank. (*Hint*: The answer is on the second page of the Help section.)

   Overlays act much like conventional ____________________.

5. Write down the approximate longitude of the western-most point in Canada. (*Hint*: It is also the eastern-most point in Alaska.) ___________________________________

6. Write down the name of the underlay setting for the January 1982 surface temperature dataset. ____

7. What is the name of the country and state located at 78.75° E longitude, 16.25° N latitude?

____

8. What was the average (mean) temperature in Iceland in January 1982? ___________

9. Is most of the area where it is above 78° land or water?

____

10. Would it be easier to answer Question 9 now? Would you like to change your answer to Question 9?

____

11. What is the total area of the selected land where the average temperature was above 78° in January 1982? ___________________________

12. What is the difference between the average (mean) temperatures of the entire Northern hemisphere (everything north of 0 latitudes) for July 1982 and January 1982?

____

13. Based on the information in these two datasets, what is the area of the globe where the average temperature *never* drops below freezing?

____

Write in your own words how you arrived at this answer:

____

____

____

____

____

14. What is the area of the globe where the temperature is *always* below freezing?

____

Write in your own words how you arrived at this answer:

____

____

____

____

Meeting the Demand for Energy

Essential Question: *How are population growth and increasing wealth affecting world demand for energy?*

Read the following passage and answer the analysis questions.

Reading

Energy use has changed greatly in the past 200 years. Before the Industrial Revolution started in the late 1700s, people mostly used firewood and sunlight for their energy needs. The technology developed since then has increased our use of coal, oil, and other fossil fuels. Now we rely on these forms of energy much more than on fire and sunlight.

Scientists predict the demand for energy to grow over the next fifty years for several reasons. As human population grows, the demand for energy is expected to increase to support the additional people. More energy will be needed to heat and cool homes, for cooking, and to fuel cars and trucks. Even though Florida is a warm climate and does not use much energy for heating, people in Florida still need energy for cooking, transportation, industry, and cooling. So, as more people move to Florida, the demand for energy in Florida is increasing. The same is true for the global population growth.

In addition to rising populations, energy demand is also rising because people's lives are changing. Human society today is using more energy per person than at any time in the past. All over the world, more people own and drive cars. More people use air conditioning. Homes are larger, requiring additional energy. More products are made which require energy to be produced, packaged, used, and stored.

Some predictions suggest that the demand for energy in the poorer countries in the world could grow by more than 300% over the next 50 years. This is nearly three times faster than the predicted population growth in that area. This increase is predicted because these developing countries are becoming wealthier. Their populations are able to afford a more comfortable lifestyle, including more products as their wealth increases. An estimated 2 billion people worldwide do not currently have access to electricity in their homes. This is likely to change in the near future as improved roads and communication make electricity more available.

Graph 1: Energy Consumption History and Outlook
(Source: Energy Information Administration, U.S. Department of Energy)

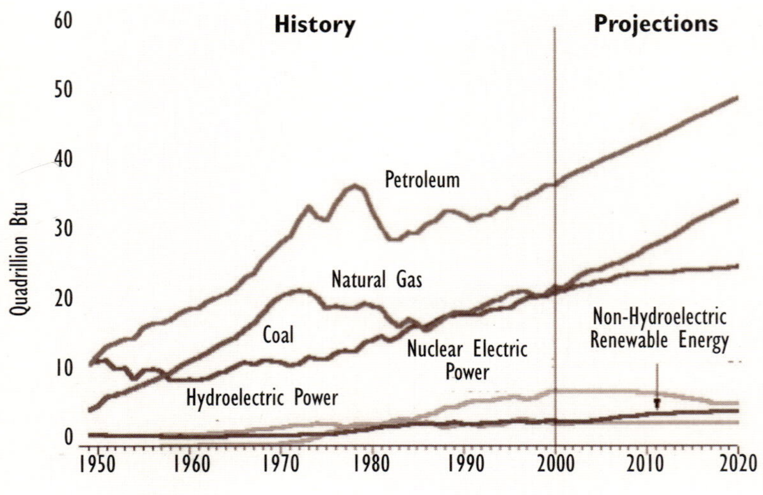

The graph above shows the amount of energy resources consumed in the United States during the period 1950-2000, with a prediction for future consumption up to 2020. As the graph shows, the demand for energy has been increasing steadily since the 1950s. According to predictions of the U.S. Department of Energy, demand for energy is likely to increase until 2020 and beyond. Since this is a prediction, we should bear in mind that it is based on assumptions that may turn out to be wrong. The actual increase may be larger or smaller.

This increase in demand does not mean that there will necessarily be enough energy to meet the demand. The supply of oil and other fossil fuels on the planet is limited. On the other hand, many alternative energy sources exist, including, solar energy, wind energy, nuclear energy and hydroelectric power. In Unit 2, you will investigate the challenges of meeting the growing demand for energy, including the environmental impacts of different energy sources.

Analysis Questions

1. How do population increases affect the demand for energy?

2. Why might the demand for energy increase faster than the population is growing?

3. Answer the essential question: *How are population growth and increasing wealth affecting world demand for energy?*

Lesson 3
Water

Driving Question: *How much water is available to support population growth and is it enough?*

Overview

In addition to land and energy, another important resource for a growing population like the one in Florida is water. Water is a primary resource for human survival. Because it is so important, people frequently end up in conflicts over access to water. In some places around the world, water is always scarce, but droughts can hit anywhere, including in the U.S. When water is scarce, neighboring individuals, communities, and countries often have disagreements over how to share water.

In this lesson, you will look at how water is distributed on Earth. You will use WorldWatcher software to find locations that have substantial fresh water resources in the form of rainfall. You will play a game called Heat Wave and Drought. The game will ask you to decide how to divide up your community's water resources. You will explore your own water use during this activity. Finally, you will read about scientists' predictions about water availability in the future.

Important Content

- Water is distributed unevenly at the surface of the Earth. Earth's water supply is a combination of salt and fresh water, and surface and underground water.
- Energy, water, and land (especially arable land) are limited resources on Earth.

Where is All the Water?

Essential Question: *How is water distributed on Earth*?

Overview

Florida is a large peninsula that is surrounded by water around more than 80 percent of its border. But, does that mean there is enough water available to support Florida's growing population? It is a complicated question to answer because the most visible water in Florida, the ocean and Gulf of Mexico are not useful for most human activities. On the other hand, not all useful water is visible at the surface.

Water is found nearly everywhere on or near the surface of the Earth. It may or may not be visible, but it is there. Visible sources of water include oceans, lakes, streams, and ice. Less obvious sources include groundwater (aquifers beneath the surface), soil moisture, water vapor in the atmosphere, and water contained within living cells. However, not all water can be used for all human needs. Water in the oceans is too salty to drink. Water frozen in icecaps can be melted for drinking, but this requires a lot of energy. In this activity, you will explore how much water is available on Earth for us to use, and how much is not useful or difficult to acquire.

Materials

For each group:

- 1 L plastic beaker
- 8 32 oz. clear plastic cups
- masking tape
- 1 3 mL dropper
- 1 250 mL graduated cylinder
- 1 50 mL graduated cylinder

Safety

Wear eye protection, clean any spills immediately.

Procedure

1. Construct a data table with four columns and nine rows. Label the first column "Water Source," the second "Amount (mL)", the third "Experimental %", and the fourth "Actual %."

2. Fill the large container with one liter of water. Label it with tape as "Total World Supply of Water" (1000 mL).

3. Using masking tape, label at least one cup with each of the following water sources. You may use more cups if necessary.
    - Oceans
    - Rivers
    - Lakes
    - Groundwater
    - Ice Caps and Glaciers
    - Marshes, Wetlands, and Soil Moisture
    - Atmosphere
    - Living Cells
4. In your group, discuss how the "Total World Supply of Water" should be distributed among the cups. Once you have come to a consensus, distribute one liter of water into the various cups. This distribution should be in direct proportion to what you believe is the actual distribution of water on Earth. (*Hint:* Use the dropper for moving small quantities of water.)
5. Use either of the two graduated cylinders and dropper (20 drops = 1 mL) to measure and record the volume of water you placed in each cup. Record the data under "Amount (mL)" in the data table.
6. Put away your materials and clean up your station.
7. Convert your volume totals into percentages and record them in your data table. For example, suppose you put 55 mL in the cup(s) labeled "Living Cells," the percentage would be calculated as:

$$\frac{\text{Living Cells}}{\text{Total Volume}} \rightarrow \frac{55\text{ mL}}{1000\text{ mL}} \rightarrow 0.055 \rightarrow 5.5\%$$

8. Your teacher will provide you with numbers that describe the actual distributions of global water supply. Record the actual distributions of global water supply in your data table.

Analysis Questions

1. Which of the water sources were you most accurate at estimating? Which one(s) were you least accurate at estimating? Explain why your estimates were different.
2. Fresh water is necessary to sustain life and must be available for all living things. Based on this statement, calculate the total percentage of Earth's water supply that is available to living things (the biota). Explain your calculations.
3. Where on Earth do you think most of the world's fresh water exists?
4. Answer the essential question: *How is water distributed on Earth?*

Rainfall Distribution

Essential Questions: *Do most people on the Earth live in areas with lots of rain? Why might this be important?*

Overview

In the last activity, you saw how water is distributed on Earth. Most of Earth's water is salt water in the oceans. Only a very small portion is fresh water in lakes and rivers. This fresh water is distributed all over the planet but not evenly. Some areas have a lot, some only a small amount. Today, you will look at rainfall to see where most of Earth's fresh water is located. Rainfall does not give a complete picture of water availability, but it can help you predict which areas have abundant water resources.

Materials

For each group:

WorldWatcher datasets:

Avg Annual Total PPT.wwf	(precipitation)
Avg Annual Temperature.wwf	(temperature)
Population Density 1984.wwf	(population)

Procedure

1. The dataset Avg Annual Total PPT.wwf contains data about precipitation around the globe. Open it and find your home state. Record in your notebook the average precipitation for the area that comes closest to your home city or county.

2. Open the Population dataset and click on the Synchronize Mouse button. Use the Select by Value command to find areas where the average annual precipitation is greater than 300 cm per year. You can use the Hide Unselected command to focus on the results.

3. Record the mean value for the population density in the area you selected. Also record the mean value for the entire dataset.

4. Create a new selection by selecting precipitation values less than 10 cm per year. Again, use the Hide Unselected command to focus in on the results.

5. Record the mean value and describe the locations in your data table.

6. Select the state of Florida by using the "Select by Underlay" command in the "Select menu." Choose "Countries, Provinces, States" for the underlay, and then choose "United States, Florida." Record the mean value in your data table.

Analysis Questions

1. Average annual precipitation in your home area:______________

2. Complete this chart:

Amount of precipitation	Mean value for population density	Description of location
All values (entire dataset)		
Greater than 300 cm per year		
Less that 10 cm per year		
		Florida

3. Write a short paragraph that explains where areas of high precipitation and low precipitation are located around the globe.

4. How do those areas compare to the areas where a lot of people live?

5. How does Florida's precipitation compare to other places that you looked at including where you live?

6. Looking at rainfall only gives us one source of water that people use. What other data would be helpful in understanding water availability in a certain region?

7. Answer the essential questions: *Do most people on the Earth live in areas with lots of rain? Why might this be important?*

Climate Classes

Essential Question: *What areas on Earth have the most water and warmth?*

Overview

When environmental scientists talk about available natural resources, they assess both temperature and rainfall. They divide the planet into categories called climate classes. These classes represent general characteristics of each region. The climate in a region plays a role in determining how desirable a place is to live for people, what resources they require, and what resources are found there.

Materials

WorldWatcher datasets:

Avg Annual Temperature.wwf	(temperature)
Avg Annual Total PPT.wwf	(precipitation)
Simple Climate Classes.wwf	(climate classes)

Procedure

1. Open the Precipitation dataset. Decide what numbers make an area "very wet" and "very dry." Record those numbers in your notebook.

2. Open both the Temperature and the Precipitation datasets. Synchronize mouse and select areas you believe are "very wet."

3. Switch to the Temperature dataset. Create a histogram showing the temperatures associated with your precipitation selection. *(See the Histogram Hints section at the end of this activity if you forgot how to make a histogram in WorldWatcher.)*

4. This histogram will show the distribution of temperatures in regions that are "very wet." Describe what temperature values are most associated with these areas of high precipitation. Do areas that are "very wet" tend to be warmer or cooler?

5. Switch to the Climate Class dataset and create a histogram. What climates are most likely to be very wet?

6. Clear selections and synchronize mouse. Select areas where precipitation is less than "very dry." Activate the Temperature datasets. Create a histogram showing the temperatures associated with your precipitation selection.

7. This histogram will show the distribution of temperatures in regions that are "very dry." Describe what temperature values are most associated with these areas of low precipitation. Do areas that are "very dry" tend to be warmer or cooler?

8. Open the Simple Climate Classes dataset. Use selections and histograms to answer the analysis questions.

Analysis Questions

1. Which climate receives the most rain? (Water is not a climate.)

2. Which three climate types receive the least rain?

3. Is there anywhere on the globe you would describe as both "cold" and "wet"? Explain your thinking.

4. Do you think elevation effects climate? Use evidence to support your answer.

5. What is the climate in Florida? How about where you live?

6. Answer the essential question: *What areas on Earth have the most water and warmth?*

Histogram Hints 

1. A histogram is a graph that shows the frequency ("number of times") certain data values appear in a dataset.

2. When you click the Histogram button, the entire dataset is put into a histogram. See Figure 1 for an example.

3. To histogram only the selection, select Range from the Appearance menu with the Histogram window active. In the Histogram Range box that appears, change Bin values are to Area sums for selected items. Click the Range button to make sure the *y*-axis range on the histogram covers the entire dataset.

Figure 1: The Histogram Range dialogue box appears when Range is selected from the Appearance menu.

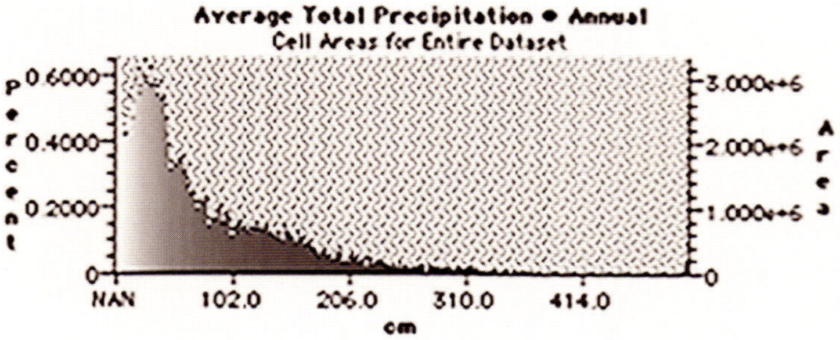

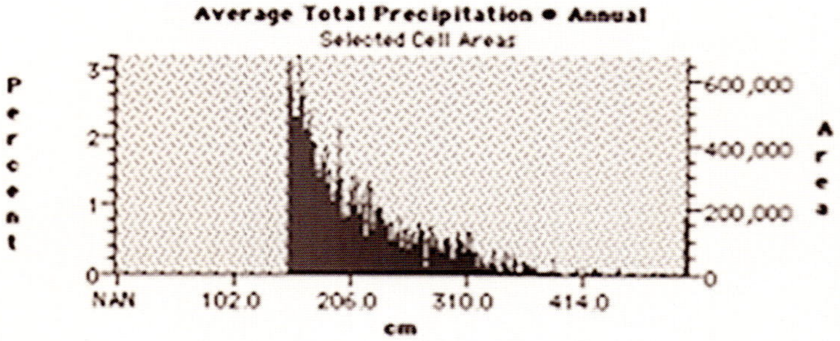

Figure 3 : A histogram of the selected region of a WorldWatcher dataset. (Can you identify what the selection is?)

Biomes

Essential Question: *What is a biome?*

Overview

In the last activity, you found areas on Earth that have similar rainfall and temperatures. These two factors are part of a region's climate. They tell you something about a region and the resources available there. More information is necessary to see a complete picture of what is found in an area. That information is soil type (including geology) and groundcover (the type of plants found in a region).

Geographic regions around the world that have similar environmental conditions are capable of supporting the same type of plants and animals. This situation separates the world into biomes. Biomes are ecological communities that have the same climatic conditions and geologic features. They support species with similar life strategies and adaptations designed to utilize the resources found in the region. The biome indicates what types of plants and animals live in a given geographic region. The tropical forest is one type of terrestrial biome. It is located at various points around the planet where climate and geology produce a similar environment. The tropical forest biome contains the same kinds of biological communities wherever it occurs. However, the individual species will not be the same from one tropical forest to another. Instead, each forest will support organisms that are ecologically equivalent. The organisms are different species that have a similar life cycle. They have adapted similarly to similar environmental conditions.

"Climate" is the word used to describe the combination of temperature and precipitation found in a geographic region. "Biome" describes the combination of climate and biology found in a region. Each biome is usually named for its dominant vegetation.

In this activity, you will learn about the different biomes and their biology and climate.

Materials

For each group:

WorldWatcher datasets:

7 Simple Climate Classes.wwf	(climate classes)
Dominant Vegetation.wwf	(dominant vegetation)
Biomes.wwf	(biome classes)

Procedure: Defining Biomes

1. Open the climate classes, dominant vegetation, and biomes datasets in WorldWatcher.
2. Use Synchronize Mouse and Selections. Complete the Climate Class, Groundcover, and Biome columns of the table below. (Do not include water as a biome.)
3. Record the climate classes, groundcover, and biomes found in Florida.
4. Discuss as a class the definitions of *coniferous, deciduous, evergreen*, and *shrub*.
5. Answer the analysis questions.

Analysis Questions

1. Complete the last column of the data table. Use your own words to describe the biomes.
2. Based on the information in the chart and the activity in Lesson 3: *Climate Classes*, define *tropical* and *temperate*.
3. Look back at your answers for Lesson 1: *Land Use Totals*. In that lesson, you added up the amounts of different types of land that were needed to support your lifestyle. For each type of land needed – forest, pasture, farmland, and urban land – list the biome where this type of land is most likely to be found in your region. How far are those biomes from where you live?
4. Answer the essential question: *What is a biome?*

Data Table 1:
Climate Class, Groundcover and Biome Data Table

Biome	Climate	Groundcover	Description in your own words
Equatorial Tropical Rainforest	Tropical Humid	Broadleaf Evergreen Forest	Hot, lots of rainfall, trees that don't lose their leaves.

The Future of Water Availability

Essential Question: *Is the world's water supply going to be sufficient in the future?*

Read the article below and answer the analysis questions.

Reading

Humans need fresh water for drinking, agriculture, transportation, and industry. As you have already seen, water is plentiful on Earth, but freshwater supplies are limited. In addition, the freshwater on Earth is not distributed evenly around the world. As a result there are some areas with more water than is needed to support the people in that area. However, there are many places where the water supply is barely sufficient to support the human population. In some of these places the water supply is so short that a major drought can result in widespread sickness or death. As many as one million people are believed to have died in Ethiopia between 1982 and 1984 when a drought struck that country.

According to the World Resources Institute, in 1995 more than 2.3 billion people (41 percent of the world's population) lived in areas where the water is so scarce that they experience frequent water shortages. They predict this number will continue to grow as human population grows. By 2025, they predict that nearly 3.5 billion people (or 48 percent of the total population) will live in such "water stressed" areas.

As with other resources, it is difficult for scientists to predict how much water will be available in the future. Scientists cannot be certain about several things that will affect the future availability of water. One is how much the population will increase in the future. For example, the prediction above of the number of people living in water stressed areas in 2025 is based on a population estimate from the United Nations. The United Nations has created several different predictions for population growth. In the prediction above, the World Resources Institute used one of their lower predictions. The population in water stressed areas could grow more than in this prediction. Then even more people will face water shortages. The effects of the shortages will be worse, too, because the water will need to support more people.

Other factors will also influence the availability of water for human use in the future. These include possible changes in weather patterns, people's water use, and technology.

Weather Patterns

The availability of water depends in large part on weather patterns. Each location on Earth has regular annual patterns of precipitation. Some places have extreme rainy and dry seasons, others are consistently rainy or dry throughout the year, and others have more moderate patterns. Patterns that are generally the same every year are called climatic patterns. Scientists now recognize that climate patterns change over time. Some places go through years or decades of more or less precipitation. For example, drought is an extended period of lower than normal precipitation for a particular location. As climate patterns change, the water that is available for human use changes with them.

In Unit 2, you will learn about a pattern of climate change that scientists call *global climate change* or *global warming*. You will learn that there are many uncertainties about global climate change. Scientists are uncertain how large the average warming will be and how it will affect the precipitation in certain places. Nevertheless, most scientists are confident that the Earth's climate is experiencing a change, and that precipitation patterns and water availability will change as a result.

Water Use

Currently, most of the freshwater used each year is used to irrigate crops. Scientists estimate that currently between 60 and 70 percent of the water used worldwide is used for irrigation. The rest is used for household use (drinking, washing, etc.) and for industry. The percentages used for agriculture, household uses, and industry differ dramatically in different regions of the world. In industrialized nations, like Japan, Europe and the U.S., industrial use exceeds agricultural use. In Europe approximately 60 percent of water is used for industry and only about 40 percent is used for agriculture. In contrast, in Africa and Asia, more than 80 percent of water is used for agriculture, and less than 10 percent is used for industry. Household use varies between 5 and 25 percent of total water use.

It is possible that people will choose to use water differently in the future. For example, in many parts of the world, governments have launched efforts to encourage people to reduce their use of water and to re-use it when possible. Governments even ration water when necessary. On the other hand, as people in poorer countries become wealthier, their demand for agricultural products and commercial goods usually increases. Therefore, any reduction in use per person could be outweighed by the growth in overall population.

Technology

Some of the most important technological advances in human history have been discoveries of ways to manage water resources. Wells enable people to obtain water from underground. Dams enable people to store water in reservoirs so they can use it later. Canals and pipelines enable people to move water from where it is plentiful to where it is needed. Today, because of these water management technologies, people are able to live far away from their sources of water and grow crops in places that only get a little rain or get all their precipitation in a short period of time. Water filtration and purification technologies enable people to convert water that is inappropriate for agricultural or domestic use into clean water for irrigation or drinking. They also enable us to clean the water that we have used before allowing it to flow back into the natural environment.

However, there are downsides to these technologies. The supply of water underground is limited, and if we withdraw underground water faster than it is replenished for too long, we will use up those underwater sources. When we create dams, canals, and pipelines, we change the landscape by flooding some areas and removing water from others. These changes eliminate habitat for the plants and animals that formerly lived in those locations. When we use water for human purposes, there is less available to support other living things.

Today, scientists and engineers are working on technologies that they hope will both increase the supply of freshwater and reduce the demand. The biggest potential breakthrough in increasing supply would be a technology that would allow people to convert large quantities of ocean water to freshwater inexpensively. Water desalination technologies (methods for removing salt from water) do exist, but they are currently too expensive to be used in the places where they are needed. They also require substantial amounts of energy, which means using more of one scarce resource (energy) to increase the supply of another (water).

Because agriculture is the largest use of water worldwide, technologies that hold the most promise for reducing demand for water are those that will make irrigation more efficient. Traditionally, more water has been lost in getting water to crops than actually makes it into the plants. Water evaporates from reservoirs and canals before it even reaches farms. Then, depending on how the water is applied to fields, it might evaporate or run off the fields without being absorbed by plants. New irrigation techniques deliver water directly to the roots of plants without spraying it into the air or flooding fields. Where they are being used, these techniques are already dramatically reducing water loss in agriculture. However, these techniques are not yet widely used around the world. Part of the reason is the cost of installing and maintaining the irrigation equipment. Technologies for recapturing and re-using water in households and factories also have the potential of significantly reducing the amount of water required per person.

While technology offers the possibility of both increasing supply and reducing demand for water, people always have to be alert for what the negative effects of these technologies might be, such as increasing water availability by increasing energy use.

The Future

The growing population in places like Florida and throughout the world raises questions about whether humans will have enough fresh water to meet their needs. The answer will depend in part on how much the population grows in different places, in part on what choices people make about water use, and in part on what new technologies become available.

In Unit 2, you will investigate water resources in more depth by looking at how water is obtained and used in one of the most productive agricultural regions of the United States. In that Unit, you will consider policy decisions about how to use water and what technologies to employ.

Analysis Questions

1. How is water used around the world, and how does it differ from place to place?

2. What are some things that are certain about future water supply and demand?

3. What are some things that are uncertain, and how could they effect whether there is sufficient water available to meet human needs in different parts of the world?

4. Answer the essential question: *Is the world's water supply going to be sufficient in the future?*

Heat Wave and Drought

Essential Question: *What would you do if the electricity and water in your community suddenly became scarce?*

Overview

In this chapter, you have learned about land, energy, and water resources, and how scientists have concerns about how to meet the growing demand for them. In the next lesson, you will view one of your everyday decisions in a new light, you will consider its demand for land. In this activity, you will make a decision about water and energy. As populations grow in communities like the one in Florida that needs a new school, the demand for energy or water can become greater than the supply for some period of time. In this activity, you will consider what to do when that happens.

Has your community ever had a "blackout?" Have you ever had to conserve water? Has someone ever told you to turn out the lights when you are not in a room? Most of us take electricity and water supply for granted. We do not think about our supply of water or electricity, unless it is threatened.

In this activity, you will be assigned to a group that represents a community. Your community will face shortages of water and electricity. It will be your task to make decisions to deal with these shortages.

Environmental decisions are unique for everyone. In this course we want you to think carefully about *how* and *why* you make your decisions. Was there new evidence that changed your mind? Did another person change your mind with their argument? This activity will be the first of many where you explore your ability to make decisions.

Materials

For each group:

- Energy and Water Cards
- Household Energy Use Decision Sheet
- Household Water Use Decision Sheet
- 1 calculator per person

Procedure

You will work through three rounds of a card game. In this game, you will make decisions about how you use water and energy. You will see how your decisions will effect an entire community.

Procedure: Round 1

It is early summer. The flowers in the community are in full bloom. The weather is so pleasant, people are walking outside more and more. Community officials report normal temperatures and precipitation for this time of year.

Rule: Round 1

For Round 1, your community has 3,500 kWh (kilowatt hours) of electrical energy and 14,000 gallons of water.

1. Arrange the Energy and Water Cards in the center of the table.
2. Work individually and look at your Household Energy Use Decision Sheet. On it, you will find a listing of typical household energy items. Decide which energy items you want for your household. Find the appropriate Energy Use Cards and record the average weekly use under Round 1. For example, if you selected Electric Stove, put "50" in the space under Round 1 on your handout.
3. When you have made all your selections for energy use, add up the numbers in Round 1. Record your Household Energy Use total.
4. Repeat Steps 2 and 3 for the Water Use Decision Sheet.
5. Share your answers with the rest of your community (group).
6. Calculate the Total Community Energy Use for your community for Round 1. Calculate the Total Community Water for your community for Round 1.
7. Find the Average Household Use for Energy.
8. Find the Average Household Use for Water.
9. How many kWh of energy and gallons of water are still available to your community? Record this amount as "Community Reserve."
10. Return your Energy Use and Water Use Cards to the center of the table.

Analysis Questions

1. About how many more households would the remaining supply support for your community?
2. Describe your decisions and reasons why you selected certain items for energy use and water use.
3. Answer the essential question: *What would you do if the electricity and water in your community suddenly became scarce?*

Procedure: Round 2

Summer has arrived! Students are out of school. The days and nights are getting warmer. Thunderstorms seem to be less frequent. Days are sunny and the beach at the lake is full of people. Community officials report that, due to increasing use of water on gardens and yards, water supplies have dropped. Increasing temperatures mean more people are using their air conditioners and thus, using more electricity. Officials report that the power supply is dropping due to maintenance problems at the local power plant, but no blackouts are expected.

Rule: Round 2

For Round 2, your community supply has dropped to 2,500 kWh of electrical energy and 10,000 gallons of water. Record these amounts on your Household Energy Use Decision Sheet and Water Use Decision Sheet. Remember that once you have made your selections for this round, you cannot change your mind.

1. Arrange the Energy and Water Cards in the center of the table.
2. Work individually and make selections for energy use for Round 2. Refer to the Energy Use Cards according to your selections. Add the total kWh of energy used in your household.
3. Repeat Step 2 for water use.
4. Share your energy use and water use with your community and record their use in the appropriate rows. Calculate the total use for your community and find the Average Household Use.
5. How much energy and water is still available to your community? Are you running low on energy and/or water? Record the remaining amount as "Community Reserve."
6. Return your Energy Use and Water Use Cards to the center of the table.

Procedure: Round 3

The days have been very sunny and warm. You have not seen rain in what seems like weeks. The beach is overcrowded with people trying to cool off. This morning, the electricity was shut off. Community officials report brownouts, or decreased availability of electricity, across the region. Meteorologists are forecasting a heat wave for your part of the country. The forecast calls for above normal temperatures and no precipitation for at least a week.

Rule: Round 3

For Round 3, your community supply has dropped to 1,500 kWh of electrical energy and 6,000 gallons of water. Record these amounts on your Household Energy Use Decision Sheet and Household Water Use Decision Sheet. Remember that once you have made your selections for this round, you cannot change your mind.

1. Arrange the Energy and Water Cards in the center of the table.
2. Work individually and make selections for energy use for Round 3. Refer to the Energy Use Cards according to your selections and complete the data table.
3. Repeat Step 2 for water use.
4. Share your energy use and water use with your community. Calculate the total use for your community and find the Average Household Use.
5. How much energy and water is still available to your community? Are you running low on energy and/or water? Record the remaining amount as "Community Reserve."
6. Return your Energy Use and Water Use Cards to the center of the table.
7. Did your community have enough Energy Cards for all households? If not, describe what happened.
8. Have one person from your community visit other communities in the classroom and compare your community's remaining energy and water with the rest of the class. Describe how your community now compares after the final round.

Analysis Questions

1. About how many more households would the remaining supply support for your community?
2. If you were the director of a power plant, would you increase or decrease production for next month? Why?
3. What is the main issue in this activity? Provide three pieces of evidence from the three rounds that support this as the "main" issue of the activity.
4. In a brief paragraph, explain how your use of electricity and water affects other people in your community. Keep in mind the word "consequences."
5. Should the people in your community have any control over how you use electricity and water? How does the way you use electricity and water effect the environment directly around you and all over the globe?
6. How do you think water and energy scarcity might affect people in Florida differently from people in your community, other places in the United States, and other places in the world?
7. Answer the essential question: *What would you do if the electricity and water in your community suddenly became scarce?*

Data Table 1: Household Energy Use Decision Sheet

Energy Items	One Week Energy Use for Each Item (kWh) Round		
	1	2	3
Electric Oven/Stove			
Refrigerator/freezer			
Stereo			
Television			
Computer			
Microwave Oven			
Dishwasher			
Air Conditioner			
Clothes Dryer			
Clothes Washer			
Window Fan			
Hairdryer			
Vacuum Cleaner			
Lighting			
Clothes Iron			
Water Heater			
My Household's Energy Use			
Community Member #2's use			
Community Member #3's use			
Community Member #4's use			
Average Household Use			
Total Community Use			
Community Supply	3,500		
Community Reserve			

Data Table 2:
Household Water Use Decision Sheet

Water Items	One Week Energy Use for Each Item (gallons) Round		
	1	2	3
Toilet			
Shower/Bath			
Drinking/Cooking/Brushing Teeth			
Washing Dishes by Hand			
Automatic Dishwasher			
Garden			
Yard/grass			
Clothes Washer			
My Household's Water Use			
Community Member #2's use			
Community Member #3's use			
Community Member #4's use			
Average Household Use			
Total Community Use			
Community Supply	14000		
Community Reserve			

Figure 1: Heatwave and Drought Playing Cards

Electric Stove

Typical Power: 5000W or 5 kW
Average weekly use: 10 hours
Average weekly power use: 50 kWh

Refrigerator/Freezer

Typical Power: 800W or 0.8 kW
Average weekly use: 88 hours
Average weekly power use: 70 kWh

Stereo

Typical Power: 100W or 0.1 kW
Average weekly use: 10 hours
Average weekly power use: 1 kWh

Television

Typical Power: 300W or 0.3 kW
Average weekly use: 28 hours
Average weekly power use: 8 kWh

Lighting

Typical Power: 1500W or 1.5 kW
Average weekly use: 40 hours
Average weekly power use: 60 kWh

Clothes Iron

Typical Power: 1000W or 1 kW
Average weekly use: 4 hours
Average weekly power use: 4 kWh

Computer

Typical Power: 250W or 0.25 kW
Average weekly use: 14 hours
Average weekly power use: 4 kWh

Microwave Oven

Typical Power: 1500W or 1.5 kW
Average weekly use: 4 hours
Average weekly power use: 5 kWh

Figure 1: Heatwave and Drought Playing Cards *continued*

Dishwasher

Typical Power: 1200W or 1.2 kW
Average weekly use: 17 hours
Average weekly power use: 20 kWh

Air Conditioner

Typical Power: 3200W or 3.2 kW
Average weekly use: 56 hours
Average weekly power use: 180 kWh

Electric Clothes Dryer

Typical Power: 5000W or 5 kW
Average weekly use: 4 hours
Average weekly power use: 20 kWh

Clothes Washer

Typical Power: 500W or 0.5 kW
Average weekly use4 hours
Average weekly power use: 2 kWh

Electric Water Heater

Typical Power: 4,500W or 4.5 kW
Average weekly use: 56 hours
Average weekly power use: 252 kWh

Window Fan

Typical Power: 200 W or 0.2 kW
Average weekly use: 84 hours
Average weekly power use: 17 kWh

Hair Dryer

Typical Power: 600W or 0.6 kW
Average weekly use: 4 hours
Average weekly power use: 2 kWh

Vacuum Cleaner

Typical Power: 650W or 0.6 kW
Average weekly use: 4 hours
Average weekly power use: 2 kWh

Figure 1: Heatwave and Drought Playing Cards *continued*

Toilet

Typical single use: 5 gallons
Average weekly use: 196 times
Average weekly consumption: 980 gallons

Shower/Bath

Typical single use: 28 gallons
Average weekly use: 28 times
Average weekly consumption: 784 gallons

Clothes Washer

Typical single use: 35 gallons
Average weekly use: 4 times
Average weekly consumption: 140 gallons

Drinking/Cooking/ Brushing Teeth

Typical single use: 2 gallon
Average weekly use: 28 times
Average weekly consumption: 56 gallons

Washing Dishes (Hand)

Typical single use: 12 gallons
Average weekly use: 21 times
Average weekly consumption: 252 gallons

Automatic Dishwasher

Typical single use: 8 gallons
Average weekly use: 7 times
Average weekly consumption: 56 gallons

Garden

Typical single use: 50 gallons
Average weekly use: 4 times
Average weekly consumption: 200 gallons

Yard/Grass

Typical single use: 60 gallons
Average weekly use: 4 times
Average weekly consumption: 240 gallons

Lesson 4
The Protein Dilemma

Driving Question: *How can I use my priorities to choose foods that will provide me with the proteins I need?*

Overview

When the population is growing, as it is in Florida, one way to prevent the demand for resources from becoming unsustainable is to reduce the resources used by the population. People can make decisions about their lifestyles that change the type or quantity of resources required to support them.

In this lesson, you will reconsider a decision that you make every day: what to eat. Food is a resource you need to survive, but it takes other resources to get that food to your table. In the activities that make up this lesson, you will look at the consequences of choosing different foods. In examining your diet, you will consider the effects that your choices about food may have on your family and friends, the environment, and yourself. In the process, you will practice using the Environmental Decision-Making Process to make your recommendation about the new Florida school and throughout this course.

Important Content

- Decisions individuals make about their personal lives affect resource availability for others.

- If they choose to, people can consider the environmental implications of their personal decisions along with other considerations that are important to them.

The Protein Dilemma

Essential Question: *How might changing the source of protein in your diet change the resources that are required to support your lifestyle?*

Read the article below and answer the questions that follow.

Reading

In Lesson 1 of this chapter, you learned that there are two ways that people can increase the carrying capacity of Earth: through technology and through decisions. In this reading, you will learn about one decision that can affect the resources people use.

People make decisions every day about what to eat. For most people that decision is based on what they like, what is available to them, and how expensive it is. Many people also consider how healthy different foods are for them, and whether their diet is meeting their nutritional needs. Some people's decisions about what to eat are influenced by religious or ethical considerations.

Few people consider the environmental effects of their food choices. In the reading below, you will learn about the resources required to produce different categories of foods. In the rest of this lesson, you will take these and other considerations into account when making a decision about what foods are most appropriate for ensuring a proper protein intake.

Dietary Protein

Proteins are molecules that are essential for life. Proteins are the basic building blocks for cells in all living organisms. They also perform much of the work that enables cells to survive. To stay healthy, all animals, including humans, require dietary protein. Dietary protein is protein that is contained in food. Proteins can be found in many types of foods, including meat, poultry, fish, eggs, dairy products, whole grains, seeds, nuts and beans.

Most people do not spend much time considering how to get enough dietary protein. If they get enough to eat, and they eat a balanced diet, then they usually are able to get enough dietary protein. However, the choice of what foods to eat in order to get enough dietary protein has implications for the environment. In this reading, we will be looking at what resources are required to produce the different types of protein sources we eat.

What is a protein?

A *protein* is a complex molecule made up of chains of smaller molecules called amino acids. Every cell in every organism contains a wide variety of proteins that all play important roles in keeping that cell alive. Different proteins contain different combinations of amino acids. The specific chain of amino acids that make up a particular protein determine the role that it plays in the cell.

Cells in both plants and animals manufacture the protein molecules they need by combining amino acids into chains. Plants create all the amino acids they need themselves. Animals create some of the amino acids they need themselves, but they must also get some of the amino acids they need from food. The amino acids that animals cannot produce in sufficient quantities themselves are called *essential amino acids*. There are eight essential amino acids for adult humans, ten for children. The amino acids that animals can make in sufficient quantities are called *non-essential amino acids.* Animals, including humans, get essential amino acids by eating food with proteins in it. Their digestive systems break this dietary protein down into amino acids, which their cells can combine with other amino acids to create the proteins they need.

Different Sources of Dietary Protein

Different foods contain different proteins. A protein's nutritional value is determined by how many essential amino acids it contains. Generally, animal products (meat, poultry, fish, eggs, and dairy) contain all of the essential amino acids. For that reason, animal products are considered a *complete protein source*. On the other hand, most plant products (grains, fruits, nuts, legumes, tubers, and vegetables) only contain some of the essential amino acids. Therefore, if a person's diet mainly consists of food from plants, that person should be careful to eat a mix of foods that will provide him or her with all the essential amino acids. Soybeans and amaranth seeds are exceptions though. They contain all the essential amino acids.

The amount of protein a person needs depends largely on age and weight. For an adult, the rule of thumb is to maintain a diet that provides about 0.8 grams of protein per kilogram of body weight. The Food and Drug Administration (FDA) recommends that 10 percent of your caloric intake should be protein. The table below shows the amount of protein that the FDA recommends adults of different weights eat each day.

Weight in pounds	Minimum recommended daily intake of protein (in grams)
112	40
128	43
140	48
154	52
168	57
182	62

The following are some examples of how much protein is contained in a single serving of some common foods:

- One large Grade A egg: 6 grams of protein
- Six ounces of hamburger, no bun: 48.6 grams of protein
- Two tablespoons of peanut butter: 12 grams of protein
- Five ounces of tofu (soybean curd): 10.3 grams of protein
- One cup of cooked rice: 4.3 grams of protein
- Six ounces of salmon: 41 grams of protein

Protein and Natural Resources

The production of food requires resources. Therefore, we can think about the choice of what foods to eat for protein in terms of the resource requirements of producing those foods. If the human population on Earth grows too large or societies use their resources unwisely, there may not be sufficient resources to produce enough food for everyone. In the following paragraphs, we consider the resources required to produce common sources of dietary protein.

In the U.S., most of our food comes from farms, which require land, water, energy, and other natural resources to grow crops and livestock. Over the course of history, humans have shifted from obtaining most of their food from the wild to growing most of their food. In the past, people got their food from gathering wild plants, hunting, and fishing. Today, most of our food comes from farms or ranches, although hunting is still a major source of meat in some developing nations. Also, while farming of fish and cultivation of shellfish is increasingly common, most seafood is still caught in the wild.

Resource requirements of growing crops

The primary resources required to grow crops for food are land and water. However, not all land and water are suitable for farming. Farming requires land with a layer of soil that can retain water and contains sufficient nutrients to support crops. The soil type and the weather (temperatures, sunlight, and precipitation) determine what crops can be grown in a particular location. Finally, farming requires a sufficient supply of unpolluted freshwater.

In the U.S., approximately 377 million acres of land are used to grow crops, an area only slightly smaller than the state of Alaska. The two most common crops in the United States are corn and soybeans, which together use approximately 41 percent of U.S. cropland. In 2004, the U.S. Department of Agriculture (USDA) reported that 81 million acres of farmland were used to grow corn and 74.8 million acres for soybeans. This is approximately the size of the states of New Mexico and Arizona combined.

To be used for farming, land must be converted from some other state. Most farmland has been converted from forests and grasslands, causing the loss of habitat for native plants and animals. Worldwide, about 40 percent of the land that could be converted to cropland is in use for growing crops. While the conversion from natural habitat to farmland has nearly stopped in the U.S., the growth in global population is resulting in massive deforestation. Nearly 24 million acres of forestland, an area larger than the state of Massachusetts, is being converted to farmland each year globally. On the other hand, once land is converted to farming, it can continue to support farming indefinitely, as long as modern agricultural practices are used. If they are not, then land can become "farmed out" over a period of years, resulting in erosion or irreplaceable loss of nutrients from the soil. While nearly all farms in the United States use sustainable practices, there are many parts of the world where these practices are not used.

Most of the water required to grow crops in the United States is delivered to farms naturally in the form of rainwater. In addition, water is also drawn from lakes, rivers, and reservoirs that collect rainwater and snow melt. In some cases, this water flows hundreds or thousands of miles from its source through canals and pipelines to fields. To meet the complete needs of crops for water, additional water is drawn from underground sources by wells. In an average year, with no major droughts, the U.S. uses 185 billion liters (49 billion gallons) of water drawn from below ground. While surface water in lakes, rivers, and reservoirs can be rapidly replaced by annual rain and snowfall, underground water takes much longer to replenish. In many locations these natural reservoirs are being depleted because more water is being removed each year than flows back in.

Growing crops may require additional resources, such as fertilizers and pesticides. Fertilizers are chemicals that contain nutrients. Pesticides are chemicals that kill organisms that eat crops or cause them harm. While these chemical resources are relatively plentiful, their use may have other environmental impacts. For example, overuse or other inappropriate use of fertilizers or pesticides can result in them seeping into underground water supplies or flowing into rivers and lakes. When these chemicals enter the water supply, they can harm organisms that drink or live in the water. They can also disrupt ecosystems that depend on the water in other ways, for example, by triggering an extreme growth in the population of one organism.

Resource requirements of growing animals for food

The production of meat and other food from animals (such as dairy and eggs) requires land and freshwater resources like crops do, but it also requires food for the animals. In 1997, the U.S. Department of Agriculture (USDA) reported that it takes 7kg of feed to produce 1 kg of edible beef. Chickens require 3.4 kg of feed to make 1 kg of edible poultry, and pigs need 8.4 kg of feed to yield 1 kg of pork or ham.

Growing feed for animals requires land. Some animals, such as cattle and sheep, are grazing animals, which means that they eat grasses and other vegetation where they grow in fields. Feeding livestock by grazing requires substantial amounts of land to avoid overgrazing. In sustainable grazing, the animals only eat part of each plant, enabling it to grow back. Overgrazing occurs when animals eat plants all the way down to the ground. Once land is overgrazed, it can take a long time for vegetation to grow back, and the exposed land becomes vulnerable to erosion by water and wind, which may prevent the vegetation from growing back at all. To avoid overgrazing, ranchers move animals from one grazing area to another. On average, each individual head of beef cattle requires 3 acres of grazing land (equivalent to 1.5 average city blocks). That translates into 1 acre of land to produce 74.8 kg (165 lbs.) of beef. In comparison, one acre of land can produce 406 kg (8,960 lbs) of corn, on average. The land required by grazing animals can be greatly reduced if they are kept in a small area and fed grains that were grown as crops. However, the land used to grow their feed must still be included in the calculation of the total land resources required to produce animal food products. Because land that will not grow crops can be used for grazing, and there is no cost to harvest and transport crops to the livestock, it can be less expensive to graze livestock than to feed them farm-raised crops. In addition, land that is used for grazing can continue to provide habitat for native plants and ecosystems. Using land for grazing alters the ecosystem on the land much less than converting it to cropland. Overall, approximately 800 million acres, about 40 percent of the total land in the U.S., is used for grazing, and an additional 60 million acres are used for growing grain for feed.

Livestock also require fresh water for drinking. The amount of water required to produce animal food products is substantially larger than the amount required to grow crops. Grain-fed livestock consume 3,700 liters of water over their lifetime for every kg of edible meat they produce, compared with 120 liters of water needed to produce one kg of soybeans. The USDA estimates that, in 1990, livestock consumed a total of 17 billion liters (4.5 billion gallons) of fresh water per day. Forty percent of that amount was surface water and 60 percent was withdrawn from underground sources. If we estimate that in 1990, 250 million Americans drank about 473 million liters of fresh water per day, then consumption of water by livestock in the U.S. is 36 times the consumption by people.

Resource requirements of obtaining fish for food

Another important source of protein for much of the world's populations is seafood. The production of seafood does not require many land or freshwater resources, since most seafood is caught in the oceans. However, the production of seafood does require other natural resources.

Fish and other seafood can be harvested from the wild or raised by people. Wild fish and shellfish populations are a limited resource themselves. As human population has grown and demand for food has increased, some wild fish and shellfish populations have been significantly depleted by overfishing. Overfishing occurs when more fish are caught over a period of years than are being replaced through natural reproduction. The way to prevent overfishing is to regulate the number of fish that can be caught, but since most fish are caught in international waters, regulating fish catches requires agreement and cooperation among countries. After overfishing occurs, it can take decades of restrictions on fishing for the populations to return to their earlier sizes. Because fish are members of interconnected ecosystems, overfishing of one species can have implications for the many other aquatic species.

An alternative to harvesting fish and other seafood in the wild is to farm them. There are several forms of fish farming. Freshwater fish can be grown in tanks, ponds, and ditches. Saltwater fish are typically raised in large pens, or cages, in ocean waters. Farming of freshwater fish requires land, but fish farming can be done on land that is not ecologically productive or suitable for other human use. Freshwater fish farming does require substantial quantities of water, but the water can be purified and re-used for fish farming or other purposes, such as irrigation.

Fish farming also requires resources to feed the fish. Depending on the species, the food can be from plant or animal sources. Tilapia, a plant-eating freshwater fish, thrives on algae, which is a microscopic plant that grows naturally in tilapia ponds or tanks that are fertilized with manure. For that reason, tilapia farming is compatible with livestock farming, where the manure from chicken or pigs can be used to fertilize the algae in the tilapia pond or tank. Omnivorous fish, such as catfish or carp, are usually fed a mix of grain and fishmeal to meet their dietary requirements. Carnivorous fish, such as salmon, must be fed animal products, typically fishmeal made from wild-caught fish. In fact, studies have shown that current practices for salmon fishing typically require more than 3 kg of wild-caught fish to for every 1 kg of salmon produced. Thus, while farming of a carnivorous species may prevent overfishing of that species in the wild, it poses the risk of overfishing other species for feed.

Environmental Impacts of Food Production

In this reading, we have considered the resources required to produce foods that can be sources of dietary protein. Depending on the nature and quantity of the resources required to produce a certain food, the production of that food to meet the demands of a growing population may become unsustainable. If the production of a food requires more resources than are currently available or if it requires resources that cannot be replenished as quickly as they are consumed, then that food production is not sustainable.

Resource consumption is not the only environmental issue associated with food production. For example, the production of food creates waste that must be disposed of in some way. When crops are harvested, only part of the plant is used for food. The rest must be disposed of in some way. Similarly, animals grown for meat, eggs, or dairy produce manure. The disposal of these waste products can have impacts on the environment. In addition, the processes of food production may release substances into the environment that are harmful to living things or affect the balance in ecosystems. For example, if proper safeguards are not taken, pesticides from crop production and antibiotics from animal production may make their way into the environment.

As the human population grows, the decisions that individuals and societies make about their food sources will have important implications for the environment.

Analysis Questions

1. What is the difference between essential proteins and non-essential proteins?

2. Complete the table below, comparing these examples of foods that can provide dietary protein. For each food source, list the resources that are required to produce it.

Protein Source	Complete Protein?	Resource Requirements of Food Production
Tofu (soybean curd)	Yes	
Corn	No	
Beef	Yes	
Chicken	Yes	
Farm-raised tilapia	Yes	
Wild-caught salmon	Yes	
Farm-raised salmon	Yes	

3. Answer the essential question: *How might changing the source of protein in your diet change the resources that are required to support your lifestyle?*

Constraints and Considerations

Essential Question: *What are three acceptable options for combinations of food that will provide you with enough dietary protein?*

Overview

In the next three activities, you will make a decision about what combination of foods you would prefer to eat in order to get enough dietary protein. You will use the Environmental Decision Making Process. This will help you balance all of the factors involved in this decision.

When using the Environmental Decision Making Process, you should keep the following things in mind. **Constraints** are the limitations you are working under. They may be physical limitations or limitations that come from your personal values. For example, if you are allergic to soybeans, that is a constraint based on physical limitations. Another constraint might be that you do not eat pork because it is forbidden by your religion. That would be a value-based constraint. Constraints are absolute limitations that you will not violate. An option that does not agree with a constraint is not an acceptable choice for your decision.

Considerations are goals that you might or might not achieve. A consideration might be that you love to eat a particular kind of food or it is most convenient to eat the same thing as the rest of your family. As you make your decision, you will try to achieve as many considerations as possible.

Procedure

1. Make a list of your constraints, both physical and personal.

2. Make a list of considerations that you would like to achieve. These can also be physical or personal.

Analysis Question

1. Based on your lists of constraints and considerations answer the essential question: *What are three acceptable options for combinations of food that will provide you with enough dietary protein?* How could you accomplish that change?

Consequences Chart

Essential Question: *What are the different consequences of the options you are considering for sources of dietary protein?*

Overview

Every action you take has consequences. These can lead to more consequences you did not expect. By making a chart of consequences and seeing where they lead, you can get a better picture of the effects of your decisions. Think of these charts as a brainstorming tool. They should help you think through your actions to see their effects on yourself, on other people in your life, and on the environment.

Procedure

Draw a consequences chart for each of the three options you outlined in Lesson 4: *Constraints and Considerations*. Examples of consequence charts can be found in Chapter 2, Lesson 4: *Sample Decision*. If you are having trouble thinking of the consequences of your dietary protein decision, look at the following list of questions. See if the answers are included in your chart:

- How will a change in diet affect me? Will I be happier? Will I be healthier? Will I need to eat more or less often? Will I need to eat out more often?
- Will a change in my diet affect my family? Will my parents need to buy different food or prepare separate meals for me?
- Will a change in my diet affect my friends? Will I still be able to eat with them at local restaurants? Will I be able to eat the school lunch?
- Will my diet change affect the environment? Will I use more or fewer resources? Will my ecological footprint be larger or smaller? What will that mean for the environment as a whole?

Analysis Questions

1. Did you discover any new consequences by building these charts? What were they?

2. Based on the charts you drew, list all of the people who will be affected by each of your dietary options.

3. Answer the essential question: *What are the different consequences of the options you are considering for sources of dietary protein?*

Stakeholders

Essential Question: *For each option in my decision, do the positive effects outweigh the negative?*

Overview

As you drew your consequence charts in the last activity, you probably identified many different stakeholders. Stakeholders are people, organizations, plants, animals, the physical environment, etc., that will be affected by your decision. The chart you make in this activity will help you organize the consequences in a different way. It will show you all the ways that each stakeholder will be affected by your decision.

Procedure

1. For each option you identified in Lesson 4: *Constraints and Considerations* make a stakeholder chart.

2. Start by filling in the "stakeholders" column. You can find the stakeholders in the consequence chart. They are also the answer to Analysis Question 2 from Lesson 4: *Consequences Chart.*

3. In the next column, fill in all the positive and negative ways the stakeholder will be affected.

4. Fill in the next three columns, answering the following:

    a. Whether the effect is your **intended goal** or a **side effect**. For example, if you are the stakeholder and the effect is a healthier diet, learning to cook with soy products would be a side effect. You didn't set out to learn to cook with soy, but it will happen if you change your diet to mainly plants.

    b. If the stakeholder's participation is **voluntary** and they are aware of the risks involved.

    c. How **important** the stakeholder's interests are to you. For example: If you become vegetarian, you might not eat lunch in the school cafeteria, decreasing their business. This is probably less important to you than the effects on yourself and your family.

5. Fill in the last column. Decide if the negative effects are worth the benefits that you and the other stakeholders will gain.

Analysis Question

1. Answer the essential question: *For each option in my decision, do the positive effects outweigh the negatives?*

Stakeholders for Option #1

Who are the stakeholders that will be affected by this action?	In what way(s) will they be affected?	+ or –	Is this effect the intended goal of the action or is it a side effect?	Has the stakeholder placed themselves in this position voluntarily and with understanding of the risks involved?	How important to *you* are the interests of this stakeholder? 1=very important 2= somewhat important 3=unimportant	If the effect is negative, do *you* feel it is directly offset by greater good elsewhere?

Stakeholders for Option #2

Who are the stakeholders that will be affected by this action?	In what way(s) will they be affected?	+ or –	Is this effect the intended goal of the action or is it a side effect?	Has the stakeholder placed themselves in this position voluntarily and with understanding of the risks involved?	How important to *you* are the interests of this stakeholder? 1=very important 2= somewhat important 3=unimportant	If the effect is negative, do *you* feel it is directly offset by greater good elsewhere?

Stakeholders for Option #3

Who are the stakeholders that will be affected by this action?	In what way(s) will they be affected?	+ or –	Is this effect the intended goal of the action or is it a side effect?	Has the stakeholder placed themselves in this position voluntarily and with understanding of the risks involved?	How important to *you* are the interests of this stakeholder? 1=very important 2= somewhat important 3=unimportant	If the effect is negative, do *you* feel it is directly offset by greater good elsewhere?

Decision Statement

Essential Question: *What choice for my sources of dietary protein best matches my priorities? Take into account all stakeholders, consequences, constraints, and considerations.*

Analysis Question

1. Answer the essential question: *What choice for my sources of dietary protein best matches my priorities? Take into account all stakeholders, consequences, constraints, and considerations.*

    - Address each constraint and consideration you listed.
    - Explain how negative effects are outweighed by the positives.

Ecosystems

Chapter 4 Ecosystems

Connections

As the human population grows, so does human demand on Earth's resources. In previous lessons, you predicted population growth for the future and looked at human use of resources. You calculated how much space, energy, and water an individual uses. There is more to this issue. It is also about humans sharing resources. People often forget that plants and animals depend on these same resources to survive.

One of the most controversial aspects of sharing resources is the issue of land development. Expanding cities and towns represent people's continuing need for space. More growth means more roads, schools, office buildings, and shopping malls. The human need for urbanization conflicts with the needs of plants and animals. Unfortunately, humans tend to consider their needs to be more important than those of plants and animals. In the past, some developers have considered the needs of plants and animals. For example, they would set aside some land for animals, but it was often far from resources they need like water, food, and shelter. The result was wild animals wandering through backyards and downtowns in search of the necessary resources. To solve these types of problems, people need to understand how ecosystems function. They need to learn how animals/plants use land and space in these ecosystems. People can then use this understanding when building new malls, homes, or schools.

This chapter focuses on understanding how ecosystems work. You will look at the interconnected relationships within ecosystems. You will predict how they will change when disturbed. Throughout this chapter, think about the school design decision you made at the beginning of the unit. Ask yourself, "Is there anything I should have done differently?"

In this chapter:

In this chapter, you will conduct an environmental survey of the land the school board is planning to develop. Your report will assess the environmental impacts the plan would have on the local animal and plant community. This report will include a brief description of the four plant communities in this Upland ecosystem. It will also include a list of the plants and animals found within each of these communities. You will explore the relationships among living things in this ecosystem. You will also identify those organisms that have a *threatened* or *special concern* status. Your research will help you support your final decision about developing the school land.

When you're done you'll be able to:

- Discuss the issues concerning preserving or developing land.
- Explain and identify the various types of relationships between organisms in an ecosystem.
- Identify and predict how a natural or man-made disruption may affect an ecosystem.

Lesson 1
Animal Land Use

Driving Question: *Do plants and animals have as much right to the land as humans?*

Overview

In the last two chapters, you looked at the human side of the Florida school problem. You researched growing populations and calculated the resource needs of the people involved. In this lesson, you will explore the ways land is used by animals. In the first activity, you will see a map of land use for the animals and plants that live on the Florida site. You will compare this to your calculations of the land necessary for the school. You will see the conflict present in many environmental decisions. The conflict is the balance between resource use by plants and animals versus human needs. You will learn about how the gopher tortoise, for example, uses the land. There are complex relationships that allow animals and plants to share space differently than humans. In the next few lessons, you will explore those relationships. Finally, you will use what you have learned to come up with a compromise between human and non-human uses for the land.

Important Content

- There is complexity and interdependence involved in natural systems. Even land that may seem vacant is often alive with animal habitats, plant communities, and thriving ecosystems.

Vacant Land

Essential Question: *Is the land chosen for the new school really vacant?*

Materials

For each group:

- animal land claims map (on the next page)
- your estimated school size – from Chapter 3, Lesson 1: *Area of a School*

Procedure

Look at the map below of the proposed site for the school. Notice the areas used by various animals and plants that live there. This map shows only a few of the animals and plants living in the area. Actually, there are many different species of plants and animals living in the site.

In the last chapter, you calculated the land you would need to build a school. Compare the map below to the school dimensions you calculated in Lesson 1: *Area of a School.*

Analysis Questions

1. What was your first reaction to seeing the areas of the map that the plants and animals use?
2. This community has large numbers of animals and plants. How do you think they are all able to live together, sharing resources and space?
3. Can your proposed school fit on the map with the animals and plants? Why or why not?
4. Answer the essential question: *Is the land chosen for the new school really vacant?* Explain.

Figure 1: Animal Distributions Map

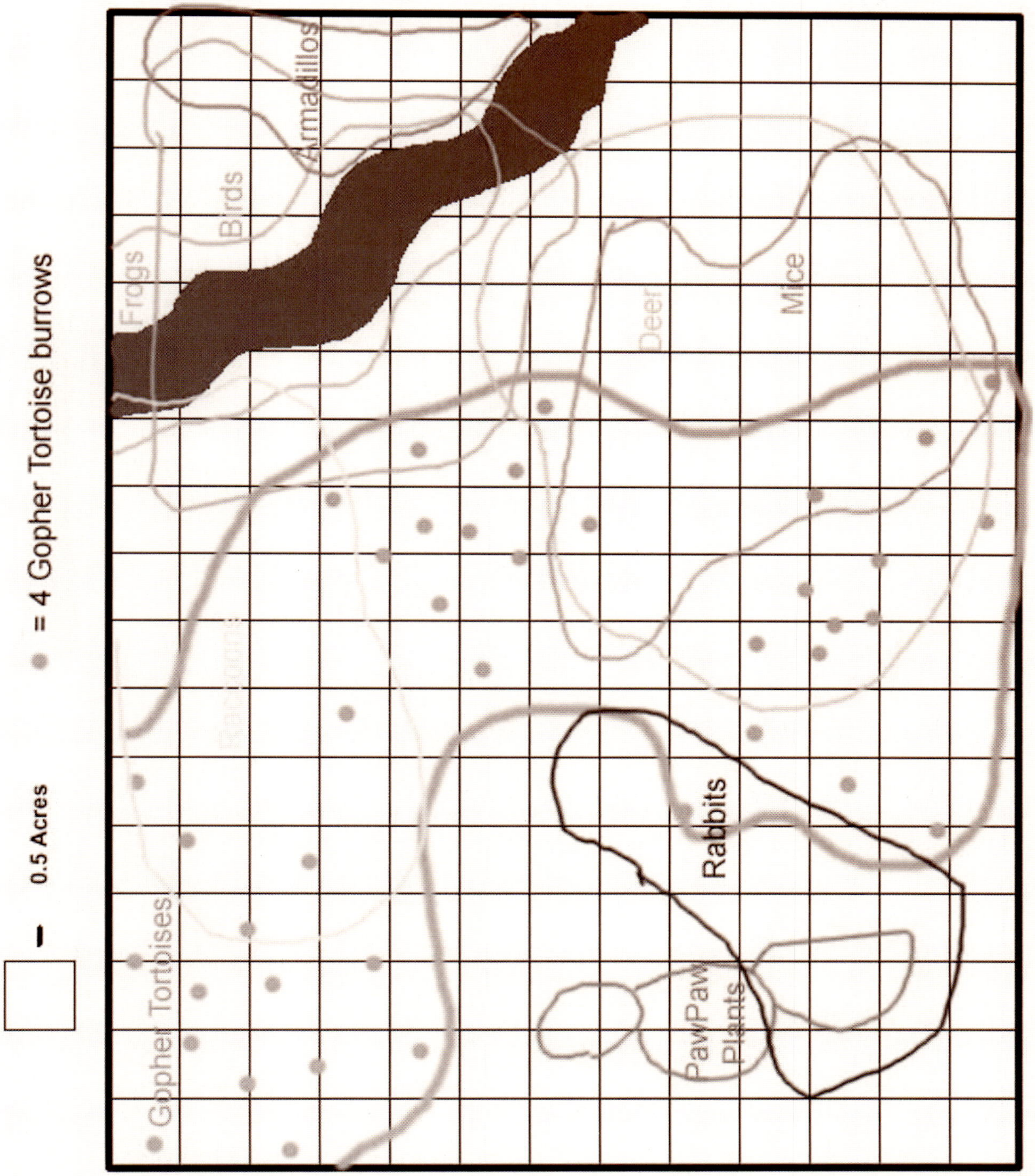

Land Use Discussion

Essential Question: *How does human use of resources make it harder for us to share land and space with plants and animals?*

Overview

In the last activity, you saw the conflict between human use of land and animal/plant use of land. In this activity, you will discuss the different ways that humans use land that prevent animals from using it too.

You will discuss how animals are able to share land with other species of animals and plants. Why can't humans learn to share land with animals? Has it been this way throughout human history or is it a recent development?

Discuss how both predators (animals that hunt other animals for food) and prey (animals that are hunted for food) share the same land. Discuss the link between the animals that live on the land and the plants that grow on it. Explore the close interconnections between all the plants and animals living on the land. Become aware of how the lives of all of them are in harmony with the resources the land provides.

Class Discussion Questions

1. Do you think human needs and animals/plants needs are of equal value? Why or why not?

2. How might you justify allowing human development on this land? How would this decision affect the everyday life of the people in this Florida community? How would this decision affect animals and plants of the Upland ecosystem?

3. How might you justify choosing not to develop the land and allowing plants and animals to continue to use the land? How would this decision affect the everyday life of the people in this Florida community? How would this decision affect animals and plants of the Upland ecosystem?

4. What compromise might you reach between the needs of people and the needs of the plants and animals on this land? What would be the cost of such a compromise to each side (humans, animals/plants)?

5. Think back to the last chapter on resources. Where do humans get most of their food? Where do animals get their food? What does this say about the relationship between people and animals using the same land?

6. Would it be possible for people to get all their resources from the land where they live? What would people gain by doing this? What would people lose?

7. Answer the essential question: *How does human use of resources make it harder for us to share land and space with plants and animals?*

Gopher Tortoises

Essential Question: *Why do gopher tortoises need so much land?*

Overview

In the last activity, you were asked to looked at the issues surrounding the question of developing or preserving a plot of land. Conflicts over land use have often been debated in many Florida towns and cities recently. Florida's human population is growing rapidly at a rate of 6000 new residents per week. Many towns and cities are feeling this population pressure. As they grow, they are considering building more roads, schools, office buildings, and shopping malls to deal with the problem. The proposed school site is on high, dry land. The land is very desirable for both commercial and residential development. The land is currently occupied by the gopher tortoise and other Upland ecosystem animals. The reading that follows tells you more about how the gopher tortoise uses the land.

Reading

The gopher tortoise is like a "construction worker." It has a shell like a hard hat and front legs it uses like shovels. It is well-suited to the Florida Upland ecosystem, home to more than 360 different animal species. The gopher tortoise is considered a *keystone species*. This means it is an organism that supports the well being of many other species in its ecosystem. Unfortunately, the hard-working gopher tortoise has become the victim of another sort of construction—human construction. Floridians desperate for space have developed many of the areas formerly used by the gopher tortoise. Its *biological communities* are being destroyed. Habitat destruction by humans has reduced Florida's gopher tortoise population by about 80 percent over the last 100 years. That kind of a blow to a keystone species usually disrupts the entire ecosystem.

The story of the gopher tortoise began more than 60 million years ago! Before humans and their bulldozers, the gopher tortoise was one of 23 different land tortoise species. Only four out of the 23 tortoise species remain today.

The gopher tortoise is well-adapted to digging in the sandy soil of its native habitat. Its limbs are strong, with flat claws and small scales for protection. The tortoise's shell grows out of its skeleton and helps protect it from predator. The scales help to protect the tortoise from dehydration.

Reproduction

The main mating season for the gopher tortoise occurs during April and June. Several weeks after their eggs are fertilized, female tortoises deposit 3-15 eggs close to home. They often keep them in sand mounds called "aprons" next to their burrows. The temperature of the sand is critical because it determines the sex of the offspring. If the temperature is warmer, the baby hatchling tortoises will be females. Whereas, colder temperatures produce males.

Gopher tortoise eggs are a source of food for many predators in the ecosystem. Armadillos, raccoons, opossums, birds, foxes, and fire ants all feed on the eggs. Gopher tortoises lay a large number of eggs because most of these eggs will never hatch. Predators destroy more than 87 percent of gopher tortoise nests. Developing tortoises that hatch are often eaten by dogs, raccoons, coyotes, and even humans.

After hatching, young gopher tortoises find safety in their mother's burrow or in nearby abandoned burrows. Young tortoises are vulnerable to predators until about the age of 6. They begin reproducing between the ages of 10 and 15. Those who survive the first stages of life can live as long as 60 years.

Behavior

When they are not sleeping, reproducing, or avoiding predators, gopher tortoises search for food. They are primarily herbivores, or plant eaters. They eat grasses, pine needles, seeds, acorns, palmettos, pawpaws, gopher apples, persimmons, chickasaws, plums, black cherries, golden asters, skullcap, wild buckwheat, brooms edge, dog fennel, and wiregrass. Sometimes, they break their vegetarian diet and eat dead animal bones for calcium. Gopher tortoises are also known to eat certain plants for medicine.

The availability of grasses has a huge affect on the movement of gopher tortoises. When edible groundcover is sparse, gopher tortoises cross large areas of land to seek food. They extend the size of their home range (the area an animal occupies) to meet their dietary requirements. In east-central Florida, male tortoises have an average home range of 4.7 acres (19,042 m^2), and females have an average home range of 1.6 acres (6475 m^2). Within its home range, each gopher tortoise digs several burrows. One study showed that males used an average of 17 burrows, with some using only 8 and others using as many as 35. Generally, females do not use as many burrows as males. Females used an average of 9 burrows, but some used as few as 3 and others as many as 17. In the winter, both males and females keep a smaller home range and use fewer burrows. Some burrows are abandoned by one tortoise and used later by a different tortoise. In other cases, more than one tortoise may occupy one burrow at the same time.

Burrow size depends on tortoise size and soil type. On average, they are 14 feet deep and 6 feet wide to allow the tortoise plenty of room and a controlled climate. The sandy burrows maintain a comfortable temperature and steady air moisture levels. This is very important for a cold-blooded tortoise, whose body temperature depends on the temperature of its environment. Burrows can be built only in dry, sandy soil. Tortoises will not burrow in areas where the soil is too damp from too much water.

Because gopher tortoises are cold-blooded, they must bask in the Sun every few days to raise their body temperature. This means that they need to spend time in areas without tall trees, so that the sunlight can reach ground-level, where they live.

Role of Burrows

In areas where gopher tortoises live, there are many used and unused tortoise burrows. The burrows provide the gopher tortoise with protection from predators and refuge from fire and climate extremes. Abandoned burrows provide the same benefits for hundreds of other organisms within the ecosystem. One burrow "roommate" is the dung beetle, which converts dung into soil nutrients. Gopher frogs gather around burrow entrances to capture insects attracted to its cool, damp passageways. Various snakes such as the coachwhip racer, indigo snake, red rat snake, and the eastern diamondback rattlesnake also use the burrows for shelter. Opossums, raccoons, and even baby alligators have also been found in the shelter of gopher tortoise burrows.

The gopher tortoise is just one of the many inhabitants of the Upland ecosystem. However, it plays a key role in creating homes for many other species within the ecosystem. This ecosystem without gopher tortoises would be like a city without construction workers. How would new buildings be built? How would old buildings be renovated and kept up? Without the building of homes and other shelters, people would have no protection from wind, rain, and cold. The city would eventually fall apart. Similarly, without the gopher tortoise, the Upland ecosystem is ruined. It is a system full of millions of interacting organisms. Their interdependent relationships have evolved over many years of biological history.

Analysis Questions

1. How do gopher tortoises meet their needs for energy (food and temperature)?

2. How much land do gopher tortoises require? Why?

3. What is a gopher tortoise's home range? Why may it vary from time to time?

4. What functions do burrows serve for the tortoises? For other organisms in the Upland ecosystem?

5. What other organisms were mentioned in the reading? In what way is the gopher tortoise a source of food, energy, or shelter for other animals?

6. Why do gopher tortoises need a sunny area?

7. What do you predict would happen to the Upland ecosystem and its animal inhabitants if gopher tortoises disappeared from this habitat? Explain your answer.

8. Answer the essential question with a summary of gopher tortoise land uses. *Why do gopher tortoises need so much land?*

**By the end of this reading, you should be able to answer Questions 1a, 1b, and 1c in the next part of Lesson 1: *Ecosystem Land Notes*.

Ecosystem Land Notes

Essential Question: *What information about the ecosystem must we have to make a good decision about building the school?*

Overview

In the beginning of this unit, you were given a sketch of a plot of land in Florida. You were given information about the various parts of a school to be built on that land. You were asked to decide on the sizes of those parts and how they would be situated on the land. At the end of this chapter, you will re-visit this decision. You will be asked to create a report in support of your final decision.

One section of your final report will be an Environmental Impact Statement. It will describe how construction affects the natural condition of the site. To do this, you must study the animals and plants that live within both the ecosystem and community of this area. Ecosystems are complex and can be difficult to study. It is essential to understand how they work before you try to predict how a disruption of the environment will affect them.

In the previous activity, you saw how gopher tortoises use their environment. You read about how the tortoise's land use is connected to the survival of other organisms. In the rest of this chapter, you will explore these relationships in more detail. This will give you a more complete picture of how animals and plants share resources in their ecosystems.

This entire chapter will address all the information needed to complete the Ecosystem Overview. As you go through the chapter, use the fact sheet on the following page. It will help you organize your information and keep track of what you have learned.

Procedure

1. Glance over the Notes to get an idea of what type of information you will be collecting throughout this chapter.

2. The final version of your Ecosystem Fact Sheet may include more information than is stated in the guidelines. Feel free to add other interesting facts about the school construction situation.

When constructing your Environmental Impact Statement on the Florida Upland Ecosystem, use the guidelines below.

Upland Ecosystem Notes

1. **Gopher Tortoise**
   a. Identify why this species is central to the ecosystem.
   b. Give a brief description of its life cycle and behavior.
   c. List the gopher tortoises' needs for survival (space, water, and food).
   d. List all the possible food chains that include the gopher tortoise.
   e. List the other relationships (commensal, parasitic, mutualistic, etc.) that the gopher tortoise has in the ecosystem.

2. **Communities within the Upland Ecosystem**
   a. Name the four plant communities of the Upland ecosystem that are found on the school site.
   b. Give a brief description of each community including the animals and plants that are found there.
   c. List 2-3 food chains from the community.
   d. Give examples of the types of relationships found in the ecosystem, including predator/prey, commensalism, parasitism, and mutualism.

3. **Other Organisms within the Upland Ecosystem**
   a. Draw the Upland ecosystem food web.
   b. Name two or three organisms that seem to be most important to the ecosystem. Describe why you think so.
   c. (optional) List the animals/plants that are threatened or a species of special concern.

Animal and Plant Status:

Animals / Plants	Name of Community	Status in the Wild	Environmental Needs

Lesson 2
Food Chains and Food Webs

Driving Question: *How do animals get the energy they need?*

Overview

In the last lesson, you learned about the amount of space some animals require for their daily activities. You learned that animals are able to share their space with other animals. They can find food and interact in ways that help them survive. In this lesson, you will focus on ecosystem relationships in terms of the energy that animals require. Part of the focus will be on predator-prey relationships.

In this lesson, you will study how energy is transferred within an ecosystem. First, you will learn that within the Florida Upland ecosystem, plants and animals live together in ecological communities. You will explore these communities and make food chains of the predator-prey relationships. You will learn more details about how energy is transferred between organisms. You will use your food chains to build a web to show all of the energy connections in the ecosystem. Finally, you will explore how changes in the populations of certain animals can affect the whole food chain and alter the ecosystem.

Important Content

- Energy is transferred between animals and plants through trophic, or feeding, levels. Energy for most living systems comes from the Sun.
- Most energy is transferred in an ecosystem from organism to organism through a predator-prey relationship.
- In an ecosystem, there are many predator-prey relationships between organisms. Some scientists think that a larger number of these relationships lead to a more stable ecosystem.
- Disturbances to ecosystems (including loss of a species, disease, and pollution) can be man-made or natural. They can cause small problems in relationships or the destruction of the entire system.

Food Chains

Essential Question: *How many food chains can exist in one Florida Upland community?*

Overview

The gopher tortoise is one of many animals that live in this part of Florida. Many other plants and animals live in this Upland ecosystem. Some of them provide food for the tortoise. Some of them feed on tortoise eggs. Some plants and animals have little direct relationship to the tortoise.

All the species that live in a specific place and interact with other species in that place make up an ecological community. In ecology, a **community** is all the populations of organisms living in a particular area. The term community usually refers to the plant community in a particular area. The term **habitat** is also sometimes used to describe an area occupied by an entire community. For example, a specific area of the Florida Upland may be considered a habitat. Habitat usually includes all the animals and plants in a given area. **Ecosystem** includes all the living and non-living parts of an area. It includes the type of rocks and soil, the climate, etc.

Habitat may also refer to an organism's place in its community. It is related to the organism's ecological or **trophic niche**. The trophic niche is an organism's place and function in the food chain or food web. For example, an herbivore (a plant eater) and a carnivore (a meat eater) may both live in the same community. However, they occupy different trophic niches because of their different feeding behaviors.

Four different communities occupy the Florida school site. The plants and animals in those four communities are similar, but there are important differences. Some animals will be found in only one community in the ecosystem and not in others. This limitation affects the food available to them. Many of the larger animals, however, will move among communities when looking for food or shelter.

One of the main ways that organisms interact is through their feeding relationships. When talking about animals this is known as a predator-prey relationship. When referring to plants it is known as a producer-consumer relationship. In this activity, you will explore both these relationships within communities on the Florida school building site. And, you will learn about interactions among the species in the four communities. This should help you make your final decision about the land use of the new school.

Procedure

Group Directions:

1. Form a group of four students. Your teacher will assign your group to a community within the Upland ecosystem.

2. Complete your reading assignment in the Community Descriptions section. Identify the animals and plants that were referred to in the reading scenario.

3. In your notebook, create a food chain using these animals and plants. Draw arrows that go in the direction of energy flow. The arrow points from the organism that is eaten to the organism that eats it.

4. Continue this procedure until you have created as many food chains as possible for your community.

Community Descriptions

The communities described below are sandhills, scrub, scrubby flatwoods, and flatwoods. The scrub is at the highest elevation, and is therefore the driest. The flatwoods community is the wettest and is at the lowest elevation. All the communities have sandy soil.

Sandhills

Sandhill plant communities cling to sandy ridges. Longleaf pine trees provide a treetop canopy, while grasses such as wiregrass and saw pawpaw make up the understory, or the underlying layer of vegetation. Periodic fires, which usually occur every four to seven years, are essential to maintaining this plant community. This is because pine seeds germinate well after being exposed to fire.

As in many communities, the smallest inhabitants of the sandhills are the insects. They feed on a variety of plants, including pines and saw pawpaw, as well as other insects. Insects, in turn, are eaten by birds that nest among the plants. Besides the insects, squirrels and rabbits also eat plants and seeds. In the fall, the saw pawpaw fruits ripen and provide food for opossums, gopher tortoises, and squirrels. When the gopher tortoises lay their eggs, raccoons and gray foxes eat some of the eggs before they hatch. Birds that nest close to the ground may also lose their eggs to snakes.

Figure 1: Sandhill community

Figure 2: Scrub community

Scrub

The scrub community consists of low, bushy vegetation like oak, palmetto, and gopher apple. There are very few tall trees, so sunlight easily reaches the sandy soil. Some large predators pass through the scrub, searching for food. Bobcats hunt rabbits and mice. Raccoons also live here, supported by a diet of fruit, snakes, insects, and gopher tortoise eggs when they are in season. Birds, which feed on palmetto bushes and oak acorns, are eaten by snakes. The acorns support many of the organisms in the scrub, including deer, insects, and small black bears. Gopher tortoises hide in their burrows, coming out to feed on palmetto and gopher apple. Mice also eat gopher apple and are sometimes captured by snakes. Deer feed on the leaves of the palmetto. Foxes survive on palmetto and a seasonal diet of gopher tortoise eggs.

Scrubby Flatwoods

Scrubby flatwoods occupy the ecotone between the scrub communities and the more mature flatwoods. An **ecotone** is a transition area between two adjacent ecological communities. Scrubby flatwoods resemble flatwoods with their pine overstory, or the layer of foliage in a forest canopy. They also have a scrub understory of oak and saw palmetto. The oaks are eaten by hogs and squirrels. Hogs also enjoy eating palmetto, which they share with deer, opossums, and gopher tortoises. Large predators like panthers often live in the scrubby flatwoods and feed on deer, armadillos, and hogs. Opossums and armadillos eat gopher tortoise eggs and young gopher tortoise. Mice hide in the shrubs, and eat the pine seeds. The mice are eaten by snakes, which in turn are eaten by hogs.

Figure 3: Scrubby flatwoods community

Pine Flatwoods

Figure 4: Pine flatwoods community

Pine flatwoods are flat, sandy, and have frequent forest fires. The upperstory vegetation consists of pines, and the understory is dominated by saw palmetto and wiregrass. Snakes move below the leaves, where they find plenty of frogs and mice to eat. The frogs survive on insects, while mice prefer to eat wiregrass and other types of vegetation. Insects eat pine and palmetto. Large mammals, such as hogs and bears, eat the palmetto. Besides the palmetto, bears eat snakes, armadillos, and hogs. The endangered Florida panther is sometimes seen in the flatwoods, where it hunts armadillos and hogs. Armadillos eat the smallest members of the community, the insects.

Analysis Questions

1. Most of your food chains probably began with a plant, then an animal, then another animal. Animals eat plants or each other in order to get energy to grow. Where do plants get their energy?

2. Skim the paragraphs from the other communities described in the reading. Which animals in your community are also found in other communities? What effects do you think this has on the food chains in these other communities? Which animals and plants are affected? How are they affected? If possible, re-draw your food chain to include occasional visits by animals from adjacent communities.

3. Answer the essential question: *How many food chains exist in one Florida Upland community?*

**By the end of this activity, you should be able to answer 1d, 2a, 2b, and 2c on your *Ecosystem Fact Sheet.*

Trophic Levels

Essential Question: *What do all of our food chains have in common?*

Read the following passage about food chains. Answer the analysis questions.

Reading

The primary resource in any ecosystem is energy from the Sun. Plants use the energy in sunlight to combine water and carbon dioxide and make sugars. The plant uses sugars as food to fuel its life processes, including growth and reproduction. Therefore, plants are the primary producers in nearly all ecosystems. The survival of all the Upland ecosystem organisms is dependent on sunlight. Small animals eat plants and use the energy stored in them to fuel their own lives. Other animals eat the plant-eating animal, use their energy, and pass the energy up the food chain. This transfer of energy through the food chain is a primary characteristic of communities and ecosystems.

There are many different ways to describe relationships in the food chain. One way describes organisms based on what they eat. A carnivore is an animal that eats other animals. A herbivore is an animal that eats only plants. An omnivore is an animal that eats both plants and animals. Look at the following food chains:

palmetto berries → gopher tortoise → raccoon → panther

saw pawpaw → raccoon

In these food chains, the gopher tortoise is an herbivore, the panther is a carnivore, and the raccoon is an omnivore.

The description above does not include the role of plants. Another way to describe food chain relationships is with autotrophs and heterotrophs. Autotrophs are organisms that capture sunlight and use it to convert inorganic substances into organic substances to sustain their lives. Heterotrophs are organisms that obtain all their energy/food from organic molecules made by autotrophs. In the food chains above, palmetto berries and saw pawpaw are autotrophs. Gopher tortoise, raccoons, and panthers are heterotrophs.

An animal's trophic level describes their place in the food chain. It is measured by the number of steps they are away from an autotroph. The basic trophic level in any ecosystem is the primary producer. The primary producers are organisms, like plants, that produce food. They are the autotrophs. A primary consumer is an animal that eats primary producers. A secondary consumer eats primary consumers. A tertiary consumer eats secondary consumers.

You can see that some animals (like raccoons) can have different trophic levels. It depends on what they are eating. Also, the same food resource can be a part of more than one food chain. It depends on what animals are eating it.

The list below links trophic levels to herbivores and carnivores.

Primary producers	= autotrophs	= need sunlight energy
Primary consumers	= herbivores	= need primary producers
Secondary consumers	= omnivores or carnivores	= need primary consumers
Tertiary consumers	= omnivores or carnivores	= need secondary consumers

Analysis Questions

1. Define the following terms: primary producer, primary consumer, secondary consumer, tertiary consumer.
2. How are all the above terms related?
3. What is the difference between a heterotroph and an autotroph?
4. What does it mean to be a carnivore, a herbivore, an omnivore?
5. At what trophic level in a food chain are humans?
6. Go back to the food chains you built in Lesson 2*: Food Chains*. Label each plant or animal in the food chain as a primary producer, primary consumer, secondary consumer, or tertiary consumer.
7. Answer the essential question: *What do all food chains have in common?*

Energy in Ecosystems

Essential Question: *How is energy distributed among trophic levels?*

Overview

You have learned about predator-prey relationships and trophic levels within ecosystems. You have been introduced to the idea of energy flow within an ecosystem. In this lesson, you are going to take a closer look at how energy flows through an ecosystem. You will study where energy is stored and how much is available at each trophic level. You will look at the number of individual organisms within each trophic level. You will also seek a correlation between stored energy and population.

Energy moves between trophic levels when animals eat plants and animals eat other animals. Energy transfer among these trophic levels is not very efficient. The amount of energy transferred from a lower trophic level to a higher one is limited. This explains why an ecosystem has lots of rabbits and few mountain lions. In this lesson, you will learn why the transfer of energy leads to uneven distributions of plants and animals in the world.

Materials

For each group:

- 6 32 oz. clear plastic cups

Procedure

Rules:

1. Each student represents an organism (plant or animal) in a food chain.
2. Each organism gets one full cup of water. Each organism needs a full cup of water (energy) to survive. If you have less than a full cup of water, you cannot survive.
3. Only the Sun provides energy to primary producers. Consumers must get their energy from primary producers or other consumers.
4. After you get energy from a consumer or producer, stand in line behind them.

Round 1: Half of Your Energy is Transferred

In Round 1, only half of your energy can be transferred to the next trophic level. The rest of the energy is used up as you grow and move around. Primary producers get all of their energy from the Sun. They can pass half of that on to a primary consumer. Your teacher will explain the procedure to you.

1. With 12 producers, how many primary consumers can survive?
2. How many secondary consumers can survive? Tertiary consumers?
3. Draw a pyramid to show how many plants or animals are in each trophic level.

Round 2: A Quarter of Your Energy is Transferred

1. With 12 producers, how many primary consumers can survive?
2. How many secondary consumers can survive? How many tertiary consumers can survive?
3. Draw a pyramid to show how many plants or animals are in each trophic level.
4. Re-assign trophic level roles in the class so you now have 16 producers. How many consumers can there be at each trophic level? Draw a pyramid to show the number of organisms in each trophic level.

Analysis Questions

1. Only about 10 percent of energy in one level is really passed on to the next trophic level. How would that change the pyramids you drew?
2. Would it be an advantage for an animal to be able to eat both plants and animals? Why?
3. Sketch a pyramid for the following two food chains. Keep in mind that only 10 percent of the energy in one trophic level passes to the next.
   a. Corn → humans
   b. Corn → cows → humans
4. How do the two pyramids you drew for Question 3 relate to your choice of protein in your diet in Chapter 3, Lesson 4: *The Protein Dilemma*
5. What can energy pyramids tell us about carrying capacity?
6. Answer the essential question: *How is energy distributed among trophic levels?*

Biomagnification

Essential Question: *Why are animals at the top of the food chain more vulnerable to pollution than those at lower trophic levels?*

Overview

In the previous lesson, you learned how energy is transferred among organisms in an ecosystem. An ecosystem is an open system because energy is constantly entering the system in the form of sunlight. The energy then leaves the system through the metabolism (the chemical processes that produce energy) of animals and plants. You probably noticed the pattern of energy transfer in this system: How the number of organisms in each trophic level decreases as you go up the food pyramid.

Plants transfer one-tenth (0.1) of their energy to primary consumers. Primary consumers transfer one-tenth of the energy they take in (0.01 of the original energy in plants) to secondary consumers. Tertiary consumers get one-tenth (0.001) of that. When a tertiary consumer eats a secondary consumer, it is indirectly eating the primary consumers that the secondary consumer ate. It is also eating the primary producers that the primary consumer ate. The top-level consumers thus consume substances that have been passed through all levels of the food chain.

What does this imply for top-level consumers in an ecosystem that is polluted with toxins? How do pollutants affect the food web? How do the toxins get passed from one organism to another? How do these pollutants accumulate in top-level consumers? Finally, what effect does it have on them and the rest of the food web?

Read the following article. Answer the analysis questions.

Biomagnification and Bioaccumulation

Bioaccumulation is the buildup of toxins in the bodies of organisms in a food chain. These toxins become concentrated in the primary producers, or green plants. A toxin is *concentrated* when there is more of it in an organism than in the environment. This happens when the toxin resembles inorganic nutrients plants need. The plants take in the toxin and store it in their tissues.

Biomagnification follows bioaccumulation. Biomagnification is the increasing concentration of these toxins as they are passed on in the food chain. For example, a toxin absorbed by the primary producers, such as a plant, is passed on to the primary consumers. Primary consumers eat many plants, so they ingest lots of the toxins: the toxins get stored in the fat of the consumers body. When primary consumers are eaten by the secondary consumers, the secondary consumers ingest the toxins from all the plants the primary consumer ate. Tertiary consumers eat many secondary consumers and ingest toxins from all lower trophic levels. This is equal to the toxins from thousands of plants. Thus, toxins become highly concentrated in animals at the highest trophic levels. These toxins can reach harmful levels and even kill the top-level organisms.

Some toxins are short-lived. These toxins can be broken down into harmless substances in an organism that ingests it. This prevents the toxin from being passed on. Some toxins are not mobile. They do not easily move through the environment. It is harder for organisms to get to these toxins and consume them. These toxins also do not enter the food chain. Some toxins are soluble in water instead of fat. The toxins will leave the organism's body through sweat and urine and also not enter the food chain. The harmful toxins are fat-soluble. They remain stored in the fat of the organism. If the toxin is not biologically active, it will accumulate but not harm the organism.

In order for biomagnification to occur, a toxin must meet four conditions:

1. It must be long-lived.
2. It must be mobile.
3. It must be soluble in body fats.
4. It must be biologically active (harmful to the organism).

Figure 1: Concentration of DDT in a food chain

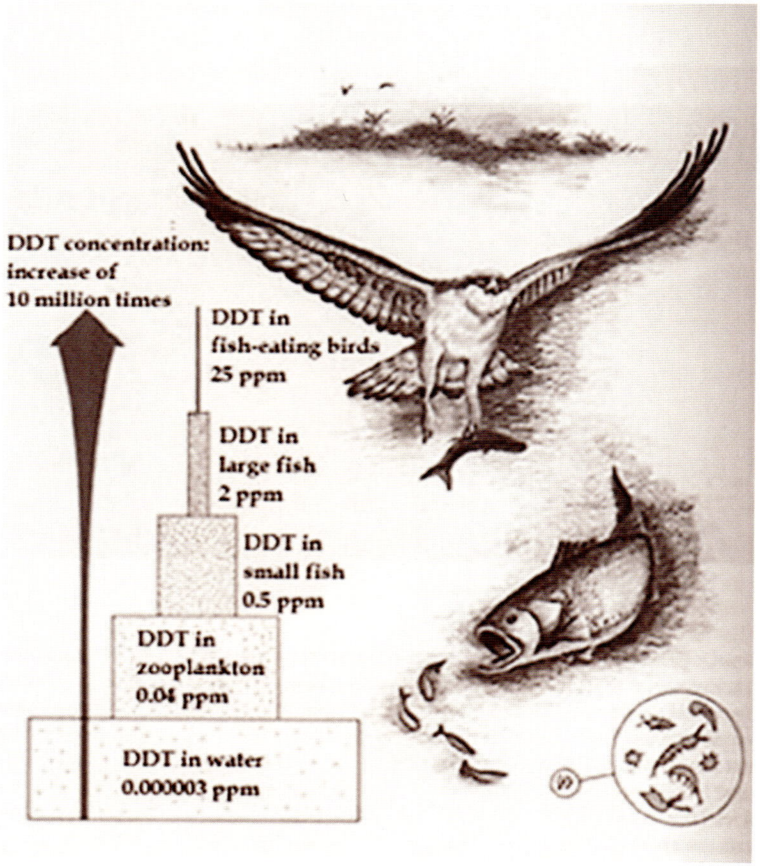

An Example

A classic example of biomagnification involves birds and the chemical DDT. DDT is an insecticide that was used for many years in the U.S. before it was discovered to be toxic. DDT, or dichlorodiphenyltrichlorethane was first used in the mid-1900s to kill mosquitoes.

Certain mosquitoes carry malaria, an often deadly disease common in tropical countries. Prior to DDT, there was little protection against disease-carrying mosquitoes and the disease was rampant. To control the mosquito population, huge quantities of DDT were sprayed over wet areas where disease-carrying mosquitoes bred. The DDT washed into streams, and eventually into lakes and rivers. At first, its effects went unnoticed. The DDT was ingested by zooplankton—tiny water animals—from the bottom of the lakes and rivers. At this point, DDT was at relatively low concentrations.

Fish then ate the zooplankton. Fish have to eat a lot of zooplankton to survive. So the fish consumed a greater concentration of DDT because they got some from each zooplankton they ate. Suppose, for example, each zooplankton contains 1 bit of DDT. It passes one-tenth of it (0.1 bits) on to fish. If each fish eats 1,000 zooplankton a day, it is ingesting 100 bits of DDT daily. The DDT gets stored in the fish's fatty tissues. Over its lifetime, the fish will feed on more zooplankton and huge quantities of DDT will accumulate in the fish. However, the DDT did not yet show signs of harming the contaminated fish.

Further up the food web, the contaminated fish are eaten by predator birds like eagles and ospreys. Over an eagle's lifetime, it will prey upon more and more fish, thus increasing its level of DDT every time it feeds. For example, suppose an eagle eats two one-year-old fish per day. Each young fish contains 36,500 bits of DDT. So one eagle ingests 73,000 bits of DDT daily and it is stored in the bird's body. By the time it gets to organisms at the top of the trophic food chain, the amount of DDT has increased tremendously. Another problem with DDT is that it stays in the environment for decades.

By the 1960s, eagles and ospreys were seriously threatened. The DDT in their bodies caused females to produce eggs with extremely thin shells. The populations of these birds declined because shells broke during incubation. Since the banning of DDT, these bird species have recovered and their numbers have increased.

A similar process may be occurring in the Florida Upland ecosystem where raccoons feed on large fish and Florida panthers feed on raccoons. Conservationists are concerned about the panther because high levels of DDT can be passed from the fish to the raccoons and on to the highly endangered panther.

Analysis Questions

1. In what trophic level does bioaccumulation occur?
2. Is biomagnification the process of animals producing more of the toxin? If not, how does biomagnification work?
3. Answer the essential question: *Why are animals at the top of the food chain more vulnerable to pollution than those at lower trophic levels?*

Food Chains to Food Webs

Essential Question: *How do food webs help us understand an ecosystem?*

Overview

You have learned that many animals can be found in more than one food chain. The linear design of the food chain model is useful for looking at one particular pathway of energy transfer. This model is not as helpful when looking at energy flow through the whole ecosystem. An ecosystem's survival is based on its interconnections. Having plants and animals in multiple food chains helps the ecosystem survive during difficult conditions. If animal A had only one food source and something happened to that food source, all the animals connected to animal A on the food chain would suffer or die out. Having multiple food sources is a built-in safety net for the survival of many organisms.

In this lesson, you are going to build a visual model. It will include all the predator–prey and producer–consumer relationships in an ecosystem. Scientists call these interconnections a food web. A food web is a network of overlapping, interlinked food chains. A food web includes primary producers, and many different consumers and decomposers.

You will build one food web per group.

Materials

For each student:

- the sheet that contains all of your food chains created in Lesson 2: *Food Chains*
- scenario paragraphs from Lesson 2: *Food Chains*

Safety Concerns

Return all materials as instructed by your teacher.

Procedure

1. You will be building a group food web using all of the food chains you created in Lesson 2: *Food Chains*. Use the community descriptions from *Food Chains* to help you create your food webs.
2. On the next page, there is a blank diagram with the names of all the animals in the Florida Upland ecosystem. Find the animals that are mentioned in the food chains you created.
3. Use arrows to connect the different plants and animals from your food chains. Make sure your arrows are pointing from the eaten organism to the organism that eats it. These arrows represent the direction of energy flow in the ecosystem.
4. You will notice that many plants and animals are part of several food chains.

Analysis Questions

1. What is the difference between a food chain and food web?
2. In your class, does every food web look the same? Why or why not?
3. How many food chains can form from a single primary producer?
4. At how many trophic levels does a bear feed? A panther?
5. Suppose an animal has many connections to other animals in a food web. What does that mean about the importance of that animal to the ecosystem?
6. Could humans ever be a part of a food web? Why or why not?
7. Answer the essential question: *How do food webs help us understand an ecosystem?*

*Reminder: You should continue to fill out your *Ecosystem Fact Sheet* (from Lesson 1: *Ecosystems Land Notes*). After this lesson, you should answer Questions 3a and 3b.

Figure 1: Upland Ecosystem Food Webs

Pine

Rabbit

Mouse

Bear

Palmetto Berries

Snake

Frog

Insect

Armadillo

Saw Pawpaw

Opossum

Bird

Gopher Apple

GOPHER TORTOISE

Panther

Deer

Hog

Oak

Bobcat

Raccoon

Wiregrass

Squirrel

Fox

Disturbances to Food Webs

Essential Question: *If a food web has many members and many connections, is it more or less able to survive disturbances?*

Overview

In this unit, you have focused on the interconnections of the Florida Upland ecosystem. You have learned about its organisms, their relationships, and their environment. In this activity, you will see how disturbances can affect a food web and populations from a different ecosystem. Sources of disturbances include disease, human development, migration, flood, and other natural disasters.

Analysis Questions

1. Look at the food web below from a river in the Pacific Northwest.

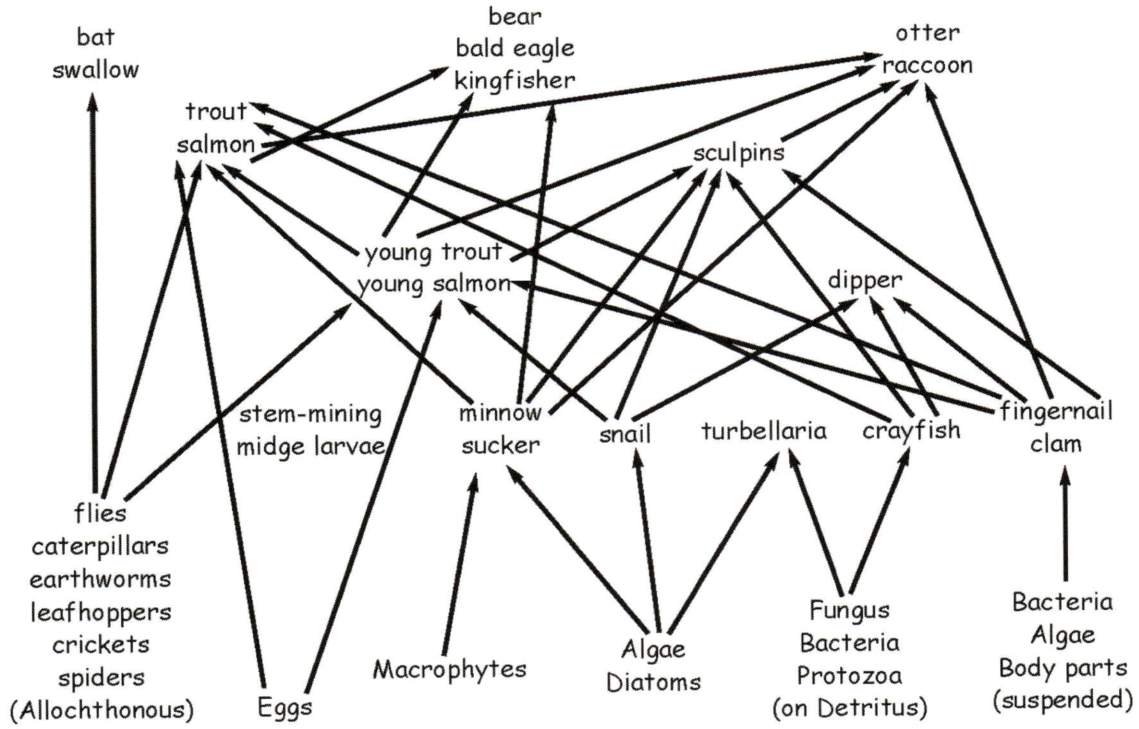

Figure 1: Pacific Northwest Food Webs

a. What would happen to the otter population if there were no trout and salmon to eat?

b. What organisms would be affected if the sculpin population was wiped out by disease?

c. How might the salmon population change if all of the bears were killed by hunters?

2. Look at the simple food web from St. Matthew Island. (You read about this island in Chapter 2, Lesson 4: *Reindeer on St. Matthew Island.*)

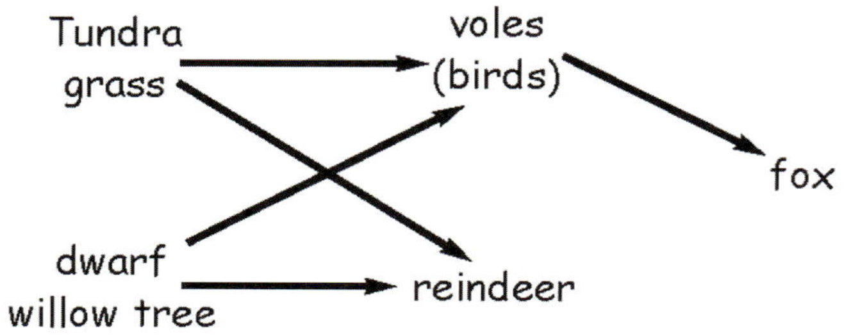

   a. What would happen to the fox population if disease wiped out all of the voles?

   b. If the reindeer population grew and ate more grass and willow leaves, how might this affect the voles?

   c. How would the ecosystem change if wolves, which eat reindeer, were introduced onto the island?

3. Look at the food web from the Upland Ecosystem you created in Lesson 2: *Food Chains to Food Webs.*

   a. If the snake population decreased greatly, would raccoons be able to find enough to eat?

   b. If the panther population increased due to conservation efforts, what animals would be affected? How would they be affected?

   c. If gopher tortoises disappeared from the ecosystem, which organisms would be affected? How would they be affected?

4. Answer the essential question: *If a food web has many members and many connections, is it more or less able to survive disturbances?*

Lesson 3
Interdependent Relationships

Driving Question: *How do animals interact when they're not eating each other?*

Overview

There are many kinds of relationships within ecosystems. You have focused on the producer-consumer and predator–prey relationships. These relationships concern how energy flows through ecosystems. There are other relationships where organisms benefit from one another. Sometimes, one organism directly affects the survival of another organism. In this lesson, you will examine the relationships that are essential for the survival of the ecosystem.

You will play a game to show the importance of each animal in an ecosystem. You will read about different types of relationships and locate them in the Florida Upland ecosystem. You will discuss strategies for saving the gopher tortoise. You will also decide if it is important to save the rest of the ecosystem to protect the tortoise.

Important Content

- Animals and plants are interconnected in ecosystems in ways other than energy transfer. These relationships can be beneficial or harmful to the organisms involved. Non-living parts of the ecosystem (like fire) can also be part of these relationships.
- Disturbances to ecosystems (including loss of a species, disease, and pollution) can be man-made or natural. These disturbances can cause small problems in the relationships or the complete destruction of the system.

Everyone Has a Role

Essential Question: *What can happen to an ecosystem if one niche is not filled?*

Overview

Ecosystems are very complex systems. They survive on the relationships among their inhabitants. Everything is related to something in an ecosystem. In the last lesson, you studied energy relationships. In this lesson, you will look at other types of relationships. You will see how animals that do not eat each other are still dependent on each other. The role that an organism has in an ecosystem is called its niche. This includes its energy transfer and its relationships with other organisms and non-living things. In today's activity, you will see what happens when a niche in an ecosystem is not filled.

Materials

for each group:

- 1 pair of scissors
- tape
- 5 pieces of scrap paper
- ruler
- pencil

Safety Concerns

Use caution with sharp scissors; return all materials as instructed by your teacher.

Procedure

Round 1

1. Form a group of four students. As a group, try to make as many "X"s as you can in five minutes.

2. An "X" is made by cutting out two pieces of paper, each 3 inches long and 1 inch wide. Then tape the strips of paper into an "X" shape.

3. Each person in your group will have one specific task in the creation of the "X"s. One person will measure the dimensions with a ruler. Another will mark the ruler measurements with a pencil. A third will cut the paper along the pencil marks. The fourth will tape the strips of paper into the "X" shape.

4. Remember you have a limited amount of time. You are competing with the other groups in your class to see who can make the most "X"s.
5. On your teacher's command, begin making "X"s.
6. When Round 1 is over, count the number of "X"s your group made. Share your results with the rest of the class.

Class Discussion Questions

1. Would you have been able to do your job if the other members of your team were not there to do their jobs?
2. Could you have done the job faster if you had another person working with you? What job would that person need to do?
3. Do you think this activity reflects the interactions in an ecosystem? Why or why not?

Round 2

1. Your teacher will instruct one of the group members to sit out this round.
2. Clear away everything from Round 1, including the "X"s you already made.
3. During this round, follow the same procedures as in Round 1.
4. On your teacher's command, begin making "X"s.

Class Discussion Questions

1. What happened during this round? How many "X"s did you make? How does this number compare to the number made during Round 1?
2. How did losing a member of your group affect how many "X"s you made?
3. Did any member of your group have less to do? Did any have more to do?
4. How did you handle the problem?

Analysis Questions

1. In this activity, each person had a special task. Working together, you helped each other to make "X"s from paper. Can you think of relationships between organisms in an ecosystem where they might help each other? Describe these relationships.
2. The situation that arose in Round 2 sometimes happens in ecosystems. An organism disappears and there is no other to take its place. Suppose your group had been organized in a web (with each member filling more than one role) rather than a chain. Do you think it would have been more or less trouble for your ecosystem? Why or why not?
3. Answer the essential question: *What can happen to an ecosystem if one niche is not filled?*

Relationship Reading

Essential Question: *How important are interrelationships to the survival of an ecosystem?*

Overview

An ecosystem is more than just its predator and prey relationships. The food webs and energy pyramids you developed in the last lesson gave you only one piece of the picture. Some interactions among species are not related to energy. In this lesson, you will look at other ideas of interrelationships.

Reading

Animals and plants that live close together in an ecosystem have many interrelationships. Some of these relationships benefit both organisms. Some of them harm one or both organisms. You have already studied some of these relationships. For example, in a predator-prey relationship, the predator benefits and the prey is harmed. There are many other relationships that can benefit or harm organisms. Their effects often are not as extreme as the death of one organism.

The chart below shows the different types of relationships that organisms might have. They are based on the benefit or harm to each organism. This reading will explain each of these relationships.

Figure 1: Relationship types between organisms

Interaction Between Species				
		SPECIES A		
		Benefit (+)	**Harm (-)**	**No Effect (0)**
SPECIES B	**Benefit (+)**	Mutualism/ Protocooperation	Parasitism/ Predation	Commensalism
	Harm (-)	Parasitism/ Predation	Competition	Amensalism
	No Effect (0)	Commensalism	Amensalism	Neutralism

Parasitism

In parasitism, one organism lives on or in another organism at their expense. This organism is called a host. Some parasites destroy their host. The hookworm is a good example of a parasite. Hookworms live in the intestines of human beings and other animals. They eat the food that the animal has eaten and steal nourishment from that animal. Hookworms can cause discomfort and illness to the animal. Thus, the hookworm benefits by getting food, and the host animal is harmed by losing nutrients and suffering discomfort and illness.

An example of parasitism from the Upland Ecosystem is the Asian Longhorn Beetle. This insect inserts its larvae into the leaves and stems of young oak trees. The larvae feed on the plant until they mature and move on. The holes left in the tree leave it vulnerable to disease. If an infestation is bad enough, it can harm or kill the tree.

Commensalism

Commensalism is a relationship between organisms where one organism benefits from the presence or the activities of another without the other organism being affected. Consider the example of a herd of grazing cattle in a field. Suppose their grazing disturbs the insects that live in that field. As the cattle walk around, they force insects off the grass and into the air where they are preyed upon by birds. In this case, the birds are benefiting by the cattle's activities, but the cattle are not affected by the birds. The birds' success in finding insects to eat depends largely on the presence of the cattle.

Commensalism is not just found in the animal kingdom. Many plants and fungi benefit from the presence or activities of animals. For example, large grazing animals, such as cattle, often disturb the ground exposing bare earth. Plants can then grow in the exposed soil. The same is true of the soil exposed by burrowing moles and rabbits.

Some examples of commensalism in the Florida Upland ecosystem:

- Gopher tortoises dig burrows that are later abandoned. Snakes, frogs, birds, fox, opossum, rabbit, and armadillo use those burrows for shelter. Snakes, frogs, birds, fox, opossum, rabbit and armadillo are sometimes found living in active burrows with gopher tortoises.
- Panthers use saw palmetto as shade and protection for their young while the adults hunt.
- Wiregrass provides nests for birds, squirrels, rabbits, and mice.
- Birds collect threads from the saw palmetto to build their nests.

Mutualism

In mutualism, both parties in the relationship benefit. Through this relationship both species enhance their survival, growth, or fitness. For example, certain ants live in thorny acacia plants. The plants provide food and nesting sites for the ants. In return, the ants protect the plant from other insects that might feed on it and injure it. Mutualism also occurs when algae and fungus grow together to form lichen. The fungus, which cannot produce its own food, gets its food from the algae. In return, the fungus provides the algae with a safe environment for growth.

Mutualism can be divided into three categories: trophic, defensive, and dispersive. **Trophic mutualism** involves partners that obtain energy and food from each other. An example is the algae and fungus.

Defensive mutualism involves species that receive food or shelter from their partner in return for defending the partner against predators or parasites. An example is the ants and the thorny plants. Other examples of defensive mutualism:

- Frogs find shade and cooler temperatures among the leaves of the palmetto. They also eat spiders and crickets that might damage the plant.
- Birds nest in oak trees and feed on the caterpillars that would otherwise eat the oak leaves.

Dispersive mutualism involves animals transporting a plant's pollen and receiving some nectar or other reward. It also includes animals that disperse seeds in the process of eating or digesting the fruits or nuts that contain those seeds. Often, the seeds pass through an animal's gut. Many seeds require that the coat of the seed is softened by digestion before they can germinate. Sometimes, the animals just carry the fruits away, tear them apart and scatter the seeds in the process. Either method is effective and helps the seeds reach a place to sprout away from the parent plant. Fruits intended for animal dispersal are usually rich in nutrients and low in toxins unlike the rest of the plant. Other fruits are poisonous to the "wrong" animals (those that do not disperse them). Most plant species in the world use animals in their life cycle, either for pollination, seed dispersal, or both.

A few examples of dispersive mutualism in the Florida Upland ecosystem:

- Birds like the Florida scrub jays bury surplus oak acorns for winter. If the acorns are not dug up by the bird, they can grow into trees.
- Beetles and flies act as pollinators for saw pawpaw plants in exchange for edible parts of the flower.
- Gopher tortoises eat the fruit of the palmetto and saw pawpaw. The seeds pass through the tortoise and are dispersed to other parts of the ecosystem.

Neutralism

Neutralism is where two species populations have no impact on each other's survival or fitness. This requires minimal interaction between the two.

Amensalism

In this relationship, one species suffers and the other is unaffected. For example, an animal goes to a pond to drink. In its approach to the pond, it tramples the vegetation near the pond. Although the plants may not be killed, their fitness will be affected. The animal gains no benefit and suffers no harm.

Analysis Questions

1. Fill out the following chart for the relationships mentioned in the reading.

Name of Relationship	Description/Definition	Examples

2. How are the three types of mutualism similar? How are they different?

3. Can you think of any parasitic, mutualistic, or commensal relationships among any organisms in the area where you live?

4. Answer the essential question: *How important are interrelationships to the survival of an ecosystem?*

**By the end of this activity, you should be able to answer Questions 1e and 2d of your *Ecosystems Fact Sheet.*

Relationship Web

Essential Questions: *Which animals seem to be most important to the relationship web? Is this list different from the animals most important in the food web? Why?*

Overview

You have learned about different kinds of relationships within ecosystems. In this activity, you will create a diagram to show how different organisms depend on one another. This "relationship web" will not capture all of the ways animals and plants interact. It will only show a sample of the relationships.

Procedure

1. As a class, develop a relationship web. It should show how animals in the Upland ecosystem use one another other than through a predator-prey relationship. Use the list you made in Lesson 3: *Everyone Has a Role.*

2. Make sure to use lines, not arrows. In a food web, arrows represent energy flow through the trophic levels. In this activity, you are looking at a different type of relationship than energy transfer.

Analysis Questions

1. Compare this web to the food web you made? How is it the same or different? What accounts for the similarities and/or differences you observe?

2. Which "web" do you think is more important to the ecosystem? Why?

3. Answer the essential questions: *Which animals seem to be most important to the relationship web? Is this list different from the animals most important in the food web? Why?*

Figure 1: Upland Ecosystem Relationship Diagram

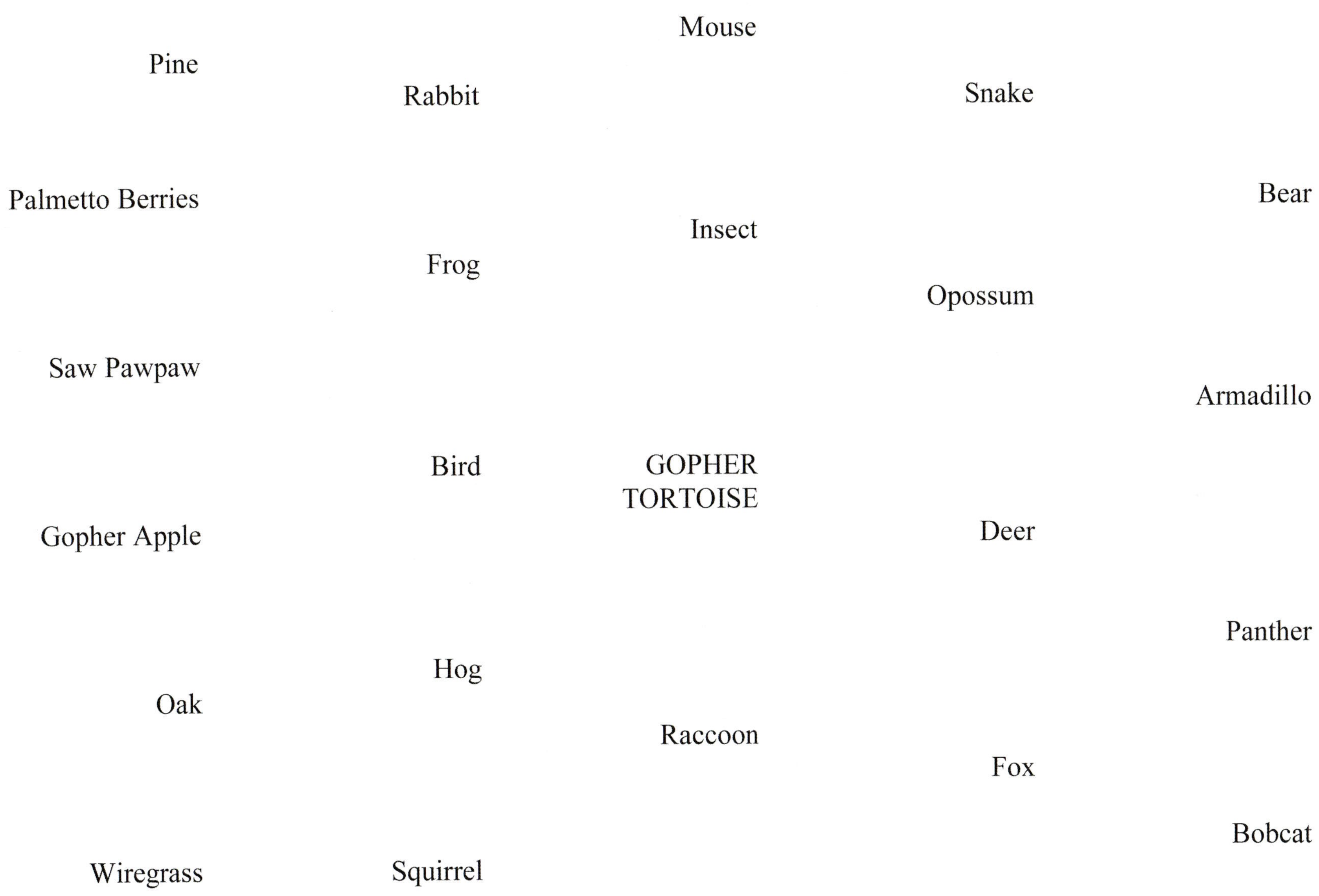

Fire and the Upland Ecosystem

Essential Question: *Can non-living (abiotic) things have an impact on living (biotic) organisms in an ecosystem? How?*

Procedure

Along with dependencies between animals, non-living things are crucial to ecosystems. In this chapter, you read about the requirements of the gopher tortoises. They need sunlight, specific climate conditions, and certain types of soil for burrowing. These non-living factors, called abiotic factors, are critical to ecosystems. In Florida, one abiotic factor, fire, plays a crucial role in maintaining the ecosystem. Read the following description of the Upland ecosystem's dependence on fire. Answer the analysis questions.

Fire, Humans, and Gopher Tortoises: A Love-Hate Relationship

The Florida scrub habitat is adapted to fire. In fact, fire is necessary to keep the ecosystem healthy. Occasional fire actually helps the ecosystem cycle nutrients. Fires help fertilize soil, enhance new plant growth, and help some plant species reproduce.

Lightning starts fires, and Central Florida receives more lightning strikes than any other region in the U.S. The scrub ecosystem needs fire to survive. Without fire this community suffers. Some plants in this community depend on the fire for reproduction and recycling of soil nutrients. The animals in this community have adapted to survive the fire. Gopher tortoise burrows offer protection to many animals during raging fires. Without the safety of the burrows, these animals would probably die in a fire.

Many scrub plants like rosemary need the effects of fire to reproduce. Rosemary releases a chemical into the soil that interferes with the germination of its own seeds. When fire destroys the parent plant, the seeds are able to sprout. If Florida rosemary disappeared, so would the emerald moth, which lives in rosemary bushes. Fire is also known to help the regrowth of wiregrass, a favorite food of the gopher tortoise. Fire helps this plant by burning other shrubs and aiding germination of wiregrass seeds. The heat of a raging fire is required for the seed germination of many plants in this ecosystem. For example, the sand pine needs to be charred before its pine cones can drop their seeds. Oak trees respond to fire by producing more acorns. This also helps the animals that rely on acorns for food.

Without fire, overgrown scrub clutters the land. This creates too much shade and covers open sandy patches with leaves. When the sandy patches are covered, burrowing animals like mice and gopher tortoises cannot dig their homes. Fire also creates open areas for seedlings to establish and grow.

The periodic fires in Florida sandhill communities occur in late May and early June. They result in an increase in the number of amphibians and reptiles, including gopher tortoises. More tortoises were found in areas burned every year than in those areas burned less often. More gopher tortoises means more burrows. The burrows provide shelter for more than 360 Florida scrub community members.

While fire has a beneficial effect on the ecosystem, it remains an enemy to humans. Area residents have taken measures to prevent fires. Firemen of course put out many of the fires. Other residents build firebreaks that prevent fires from spreading into residential areas. These measures often prevent the fire damage that the ecosystem depends on.

Roads limit the benefits fire has in the ecosystem. Roads serve as firebreaks, cutting off the route of the fire and preventing it from reaching the ecosystem. Roads also help create certain fires when people toss lit cigarettes out a car window or build campfires along the roadside. These "unnatural" fires, however, can have a negative effect on the ecosystem. One important difference between these "unnatural" fires and lightning fires is the season in which they occur. In Florida, most "unnatural" fires occur in the winter, while lightning fires occur in late spring and early summer. Research has shown that summer fires cause higher plant diversity and increased flowering. Winter fires encourage shrub-dominated communities. Some scientists believe that an ecosystem with more biodiversity is better at surviving environmental and climate fluctuations.

Because of human interference, some areas do not get the chance to burn. In these areas, local ecologists and concerned citizens will produce burns to help the ecosystem cycle nutrients for future growth. These burns are well-planned and consider the time of year, wind speed and intensity of the fire. The burns restore fire as a natural ecological process and benefit the ecosystem. The destructive manmade fires often occur so often, they prevent the ecosystem from fully recovering. They become too weak to survive successive blazes.

Analysis Questions

1. What are the effects of fire on the following plants: rosemary, pine, and oak?
2. How do humans stop the spread of fires? What effect does this have on the ecosystem?
3. Why aren't human-made fires beneficial to the ecosystem?
4. Answer the essential question: *Can non-living (abiotic) things have an impact on living (biotic) organisms in an ecosystem? How?*

Ecosystem or Species

Essential Question: *Is it possible to save a species without saving the ecosystem it lives in?*

Overview

In the part of Florida you have been studying, there is a conflict between the gopher tortoise and the school system. The school system needs to use some of the space now occupied by the tortoise. The tortoise, however, is about to become endangered in Florida. If people want to protect the tortoise, they need to think about the future impact of their actions. Most conservationists try to think many years ahead. For example, the Upland ecosystem is dependent on fire to survive. In some cases, these fires come only every seven years. If plans to protect the ecosystem covered only five years, they would overlook the effects of fire. This would probably result in negative consequences after seven years. To be successful, ecosystem planning considers 200 years of growth and change in the ecosystem.

Class Discussion

1. What options do we have if we want to protect an animal species from disappearing?
2. What are the positive and negative impacts of each of these options?
3. If we want to keep the species alive and in its natural ecosystem, what must we do?
4. How much of the ecosystem would we have to protect to save one species? Why?

Analysis Questions

1. Read the following quote by Catherine Puckett and Richard Franz. Explain why you agree or disagree with it.

"...Everything affecting the gopher tortoise's habitat affects the tortoise and ... eventually affects all the other organisms in its ecosystem. Efforts to save the gopher tortoise are really a manifestation of our desire to preserve, intact, significant pieces of the biosphere. Even if the gopher tortoise could be assured survival in zoos and gopher farms, few of us would be satisfied. Organisms that exist in the absence of the natural systems of which they are a part are functionally extinct… I cannot imagine the sandylands without the gopher tortoise or the tortoise without its scrub habitats. They are one. In the end, we are one with them ... We must preserve...the gopher tortoise and other species in similar predicaments, … if we do not, we lose a part of our humanity, a part of our habitat and ultimately part of our world."

2. Answer the essential question: *Is it possible to save a species without saving the ecosystem it lives in?* State your own opinion. Support your opinion with facts from the class discussion.

Case Studies

Chapter 5 Case Studies

Connections

In learning about ecosystems, resources, and populations, you see the state of today's world. You have seen that the human population is growing rapidly. This increasing growth is creating a need for more resources. Humans need to take a closer look at how we consume our current resources. Our lifestyles demand more and more resources. We need more gasoline to run our cars. We need more electricity to run our computers and appliances. We need more heat for our large homes. At the same time, natural ecosystems are being disrupted. Urbanization and development force plants and animals into smaller spaces. Sometimes, it displaces them altogether. The introduction of new plant or animal species into an ecosystem is another kind of disruption. These new species compete with the native species for resources, upsetting the balance of the ecosystem. Resource shortages, droughts, or other natural disasters often threaten ecosystems. They can survive only when people leave them the space and resources they require.

Your focus so far has been on the gopher tortoise population in central Florida. Yet problems like this exist all over the U.S. and the world. People constantly make decisions that affect the environment. Sometimes these decisions help, sometimes they hurt. The Environmental Decision Making Process has shown you how to analyze these types of problems. In this chapter, you will improve your decision-making skills. You will plan compromises that try to meet people's needs without damaging the environment. In Chapter 6, you will make a decision of your own. Your plan will balance the needs of the new school with the ecosystem of the gopher tortoise.

In this chapter:

This chapter presents new situations involving the environment and decision making. Each situation will be presented in three steps: (1) the background, (2) a discussion of possible resolutions, and (3) the action that was taken. As you study the situations, use your knowledge of ecosystems, resources, populations, and environmental decision-making.

When you're done you'll be able to:

- Recognize the Environmental Decision Making Process in different situations.
- Use your knowledge of ecosystems, populations and resources to analyze environmental problems.

Invasive Species

Essential Question: *How can we protect ecosystems from invasive species?*

Procedure

Read Part 1 and answer the first two analysis questions. Then read the solution and answer Questions 3 and 4.

Part 1: Reading

Asian longhorn beetles (ALB) have been discovered attacking trees in New York and Illinois. This beetle is considered an invasive species because it is native to Japan, Korea, and southern China. An invasive species is an organism that is not part of the natural food web of the area it has been introduced in. This is the first time ALB have been seen infesting trees in the U.S. The beetle kills trees by chewing a small hole in the tree and laying eggs under the bark. After hatching, the larvae spend about a year tunneling deep into the tree, feeding on it. As an adult, the beetle chews an exit hole through the bark. It then flies to another tree to lay more eggs. The beetles' chewing and tunneling exposes trees to disease and often kills them.

In New York, ALB have been attacking several species of maple and horse chestnut trees. In China, the beetle attacks other hardwoods, including elms, poplars, willows, and fruit trees. It is important to limit its spread in the U.S. to prevent further damage. Unfortunately, the only method of preventing further spread is to destroy infested trees.

The beetles probably arrived in the U.S. inside wooden packing crates from China. Inspectors catch only between 2 and 20 percent of the invasive species that enter U.S. ports. Inspectors and biologists are working hard to identify, control, and wipe out all invasive species. ALB are only one of the thousands of invasive species that have been introduced to North America. Sometimes, they have had devastating effects.

Part 2: Solutions

Tree destruction has been the only effective method of fighting this beetle since its discovery in the U.S. in 1996. The Animal and Plant Health Inspection Service (APHIS) also uses the insecticide imidacloprid to decrease beetle populations. Still, if an infested tree is found, it will be removed. The goal is to wipe out all ALB before they can establish themselves elsewhere.

Tree Surveys

The U.S. Department of Agriculture (USDA) has started the Cooperative Asian Longhorn Beetle Project. It conducts tree surveys to search for ALB infestations. Maples, birches, horse chestnuts, willows, elms, ashes, and box elders are all ALB targets. These trees are individually surveyed wherever ALB have been found. New York City, Long Island, Chicago, and several Chicago suburbs have been surveyed to search for signs of ALB infestation.

Inspectors use three common methods to conduct ALB surveys. Project members perform aerial tree inspections using bucket trucks. Forest firefighters climb and inspect trees in remote areas. Ground observations are also conducted by cooperating organizations. However, anyone with a keen eye and pair of binoculars can contribute to this effort. To aid the effort, the USDA recently expanded quarantine (areas under observation) boundaries in New York and Illinois.

Quarantine Areas

Recent surveys have revealed that ALB infestations are spreading. Strong action is necessary to halt the spread of infestation, especially by humans. As part of its efforts, the USDA regulates the transport of affected tree species out of quarantined areas. Regulated articles include firewood, green lumber, logs, stumps, roots, branches and debris of all affected tree species. The USDA requires that regulated articles moved outside the quarantine areas have a permit issued by the agency. These regulations show the extreme caution needed to ensure that transport of the beetle does not occur.

Eradication Program

The USDA's ALB Cooperative Eradication Program treated 120,000 trees in 2003 to prevent further beetle infestation in New York. The insecticide imidacloprid has been an effective and safe treatment. The USDA plans to continue its use it in the quarantined areas.

Treatments of the insecticide are monitored by project officials. They inject the insecticide into the tree through small capsules placed at the tree base. The insecticide is dispersed throughout the tree through its circulatory system. This enables the insecticide to reach beetle adults and larvae wherever they feed on the host trees. Imidacloprid is also currently used in lawn and garden products to kill lawn grubs. It is sometimes used on domestic pets to kill fleas.

Analysis Questions

1. What is an invasive species?
2. Was the problem of the Asian longhorn beetle a human-made problem or a natural one?
3. What do you think of the methods used to control the beetle: quarantine, inspection, tree removal, and pesticide treatment? What are the advantages and disadvantages of each?
4. Answer the essential question: *How can we protect ecosystems from invasive species?*

Bridges and Tunnels

Essential Question: *How can animal bridges help a species and an ecosystem?*

Procedure

Read the problem and solution presented below. Answer the analysis questions including an analysis of how effective you think the solution was.

Part 1: Problem

Roads running through natural habitats are the sites of the collision between people and wild animals. Scientists and environmentalists have been searching for ways to make roadway encounters less lethal to wildlife. More than a million animals are killed on highways in the U.S. by cars or trucks every day. Some of these fatalities include rare and endangered animals. In Canada's Banff National Park, there are 11 wolf mortalities every year from collisions with cars and trucks. This may not seem like much but this number of fatalities is higher than the number of endangered wolf pups born every year. When the surrounding community learned that, they got together to find ways to enable wildlife to cross roads without getting killed. There are similar situations all over the world. For example, in Florida, roads were built crossing the panthers' habitat, threatening the highly endangered species.

Part 2: Solution

In Florida, it became necessary to widen a road that stretched through the southern tip of the state. The road also bordered the Florida Panther National Wildlife Reserve. Dead and wounded panthers were already frequently found on the roadways. Officials feared the wider roadway and increased traffic would increase the panther death toll. Their solution was a new underpass, a tunnel built under the road for panthers but used by all animals.

Scientists researched the panther habitat. They used radio collars to locate the sites where the panthers crossed the roads. When the highway was widened, underpasses were built into the road design. Three dozen underpasses were built under a 40-mile stretch of highway. An 8-foot-high fence was also put up a half-mile on each side to direct the animals into the underpasses. In the months that followed, the underpasses reduced animal deaths on the road to zero. Cameras showed panthers, bears, alligators, raccoons, and other animals passing through each underpass.

The entire state took notice. Route 46 in Lake County, Florida had a similar problem with endangered black bears. They were crossing the road to get to their habitat in the Wekiva River Basin. Deaths from car collisions were frequent. The Florida Fish and Wildlife Conservation Commission purchased 40 acres of land and built an underpass, 47 feet long, 24 feet wide, and 8 feet high. A 10-foot-high chain link fence was also built, guiding the animals to the underpass. Instead of building the underpass sloping downward, the road was elevated. This enables the animals to see through the underpass to the land on the other side. Bobcats, gray foxes, whitetail deer, and other species use the underpass, along with the bears. This type of road modification is now being used more often around the country and the world.

Analysis Questions

1. Write a description of the problem presented in this case study.
2. Was this problem human-made or part of nature? How might this problem have been avoided altogether?
3. Evaluate the decision that was made. Write your opinions about how effective it was.
4. Answer the essential question: *How can animal bridges help a species and an ecosystem?*

Florida School Project

Chapter 6
Florida School Project

Connections

Throughout Unit 1, you have been gaining knowledge and skills. You will now revisit your decision on where to locate a new school for an expanding town in Florida. You will make a more informed choice about how and where the school should be built. You will use your new understanding of populations, resources, ecosystems, and environmental decision making.

In this chapter

You will decide on the best plan to meet the needs of a growing school district, a threatened habitat and its wildlife. You will explore your own values to help you reach your conclusion. You will study the consequences of several possible courses of action. You will explain your decision using the standards of good environmental decision making.

When you're done you'll be able to:

- Use your personal values to prioritize the competing needs of a growing high school and a fragile ecosystem.
- Predict the environmental impact of building a school on land that is part of the Florida Upland ecosystem.
- Use the principles of environmental decision making to justify your decision to both your teacher and your peers.

Lesson 1
Setting up the Problem

Driving Question: *What are we trying to accomplish when choosing a location for the school?*

Overview

In this lesson, you will revisit the Florida school problem from the first chapter of this unit. The first activity describes the problem and why it is difficult to solve. As you recall, there are gopher tortoises living on the school property. Saving the population of tortoises will be very important as you select a location for the school. You might want to refer back to the ecosystems chapter to help you make your decision. At first, you will do some tasks individually. Eventually, you will have to reach a consensus with your group and work together to solve the problem.

Important Content

- Earth's human population has been growing rapidly in recent years.
- The average resource use and waste generated is sometimes measured as an ecological footprint. An American's footprint is much larger that the footprints of people from other countries.
- Growth can lead to an imbalance between a population and the resources that support it.
- The size of the population that an area can support is called carrying capacity.

Letter

Essential Question: *What factors will you need to consider as you make your decision?*

Overview

In the first chapter of this unit, you were shown a letter and a map. They described a problem that a school in Florida was facing. At that time, you made a quick judgment about the situation. Your judgment was based on what you knew about schools, the environment, and the goals of the people involved. You know more about all of these factors than you did before. You have a chance to review that decision to see if your new decision will be different. Your new information about the site and the tortoises that live there will help you make this decision. Read the letter on the next page about the Florida school situation. Answer the analysis questions. Keep this information, as you will use it in the rest of the lessons in this chapter.

Analysis Questions

1. What task must you complete in this lesson?
2. What information do you think you will need to solve this problem?
3. Answer the essential question: *What factors will you need to consider as you make your decision?*

John Smiley
School Board President

Dear Students,

As members of the Parent, Teacher, and Student Association of the Central School District in Florida, we need your input on the following decision. As I am sure you are aware, Central High School has become overcrowded, with over 200 students currently being taught in temporary classrooms. This population pressure is only going to get worse, as the school board predicts that we will have an additional 1,000 students in the district within the next 2 years. In order to handle this problem, and prevent similar ones in the future, we would like to build a school that can handle 2,000 students total.

Attached to this letter are architect's plans for school buildings and a map of the site where the school is to be built. There are two options for each of the structures: parking, academic building, and extracurricular building. Each option is able to accommodate all of the same activities and classes. The smaller buildings, however, will involve more sharing of facilities, and some inconvenience for students and teachers. Any school program that does not have its own space on the new campus will likely have to alter its schedule to share space or be relocated off-site to a location in the community (park district space, other school, etc). In addition, the budget will not allow for any new programs to be added.

The piece of land that we have been given for the school site is home to 80 gopher tortoises. These tortoises are important to the Upland ecosystem in Florida, and the school board does not want to wipe out this population of tortoises. Instead, we would like to plan the school to allow for a viable population of tortoises to co-exist on the site with the school. We think this will be a very valuable opportunity for science classes to observe the tortoises and we will be doing our part to preserve Florida's unique biodiversity. We believe that for the tortoises to survive for the next 200 years, we need at least 50 to live on this site, and each one will need at least one acre of land for burrowing and foraging.

The total amount of land available is 100 acres. Approximately 4 acres are taken up by a river, and 9 acres are on the far side of the river. There are four plant communities on the proposed site – sandhill, scrub, scrubby flatwoods, and pine flatwoods.

Your task is to determine what combination and location of buildings will provide the best school for our students, while still allowing the gopher tortoises to survive. Use the attached maps and information from the architect to help you make your decision.

Sincerely,
John Smiley

Figure 1: Gopher Tortoise Plant Community Map

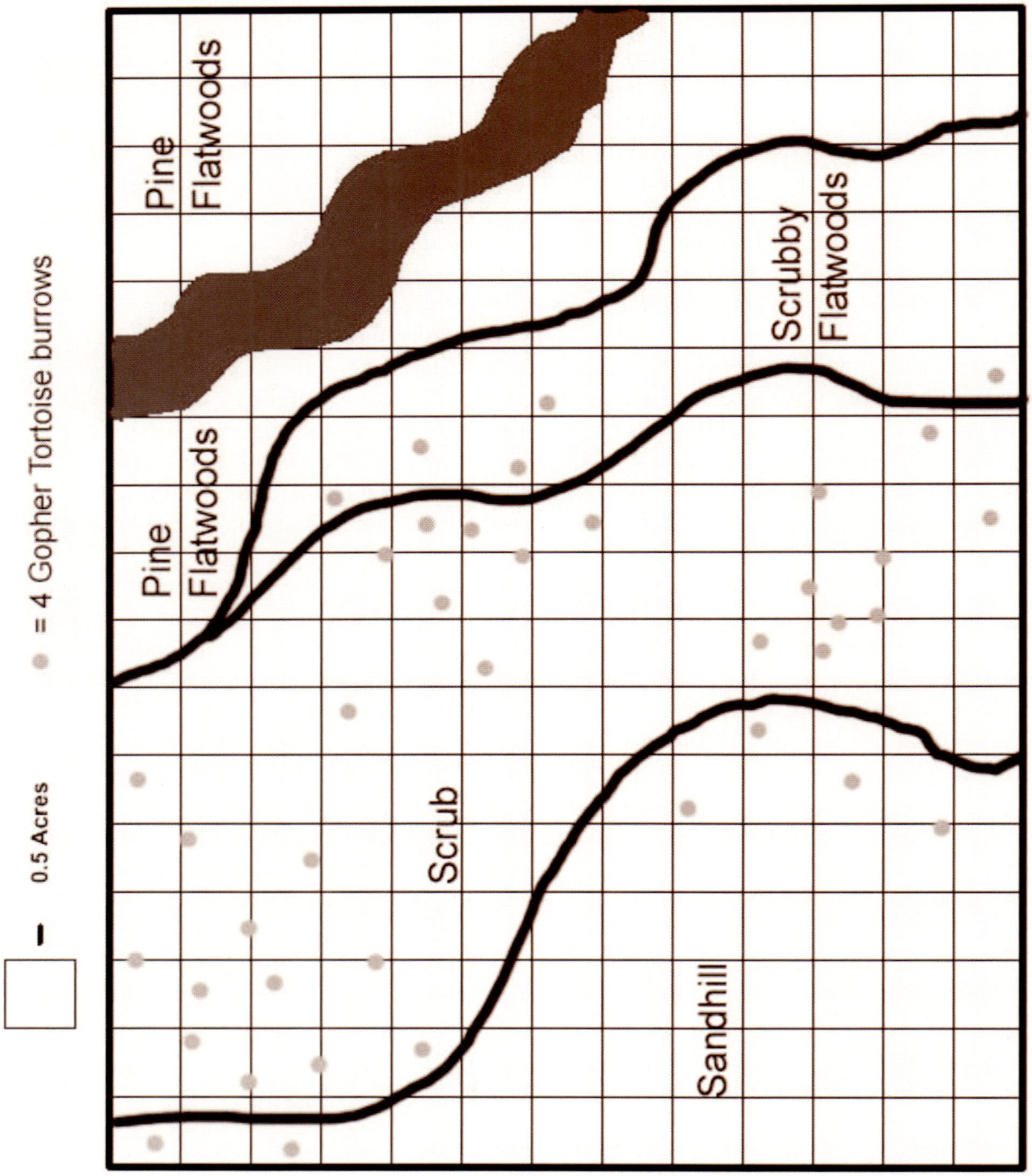

Figure 2: Outlines of Proposed Buildings

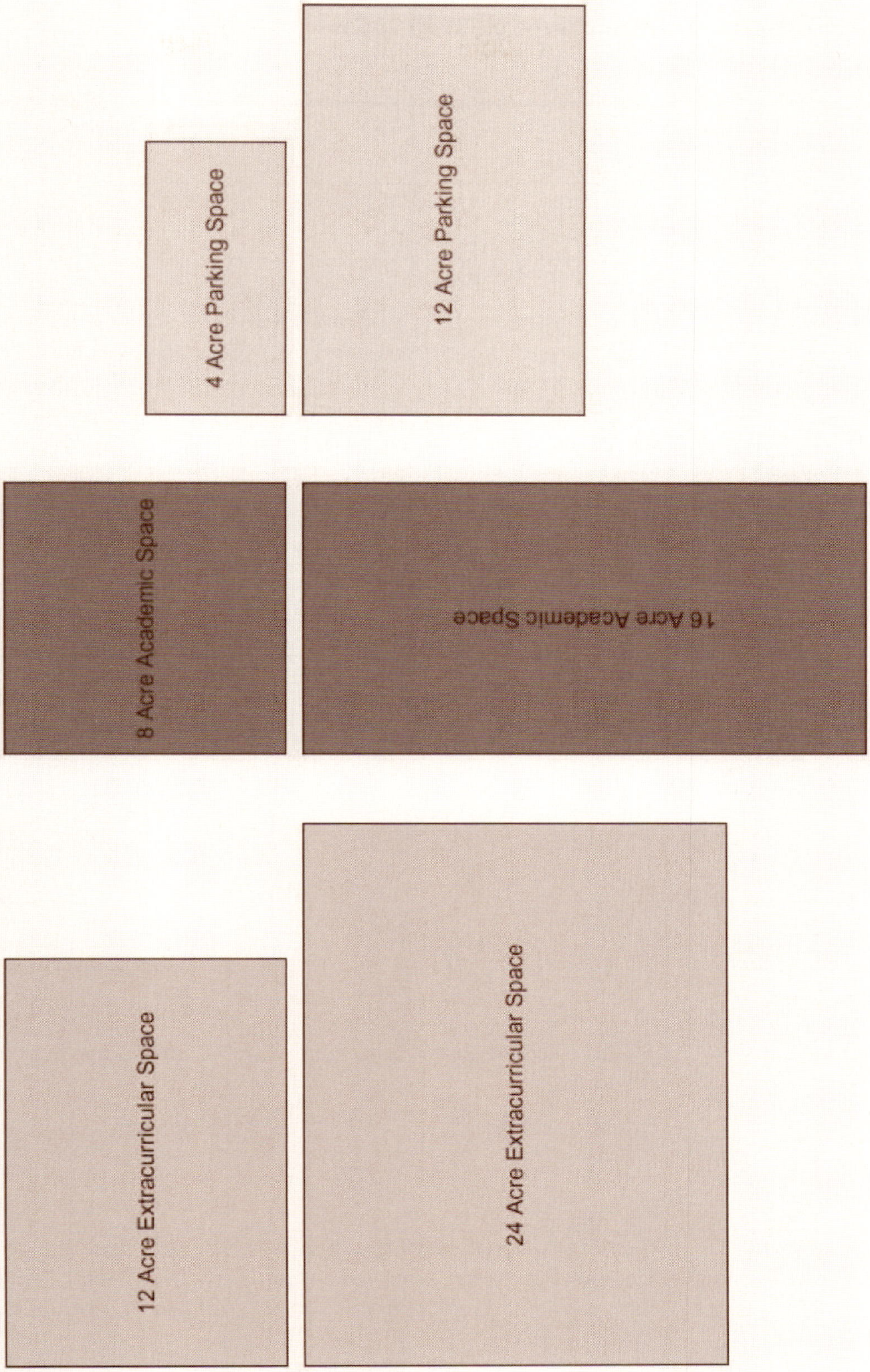

Figure 3: Details of small and large building options

PARKING	Small: 4 acres	Large: 12 acres
Faculty and Staff	*2.5 acres for approximately 270 spaces	*Same
Visitor and Handicap	*0.5 acres for 55 standard size spaces	*Same
Students	1 acre for 110 spaces. *Parking spaces go to students with demonstrated need (work-study, family needs, etc). Remaining spaces are assigned by lottery to eligible seniors with good academic standing only.	8 acres for 870 spaces. *All students with demonstrated need (work-study, family, etc.) and seniors get spaces. Juniors with good academic standing get lottery.
Driver Training	*Driver training course is set up in parking lot before school (6 am) and is dismantled during the day.	*1 acre for dedicated on-site driver training area.
ACADEMIC	Small: 8 acres	Large: 16 acres
Classrooms	*Smaller Rooms	*Larger Rooms
Science Labs	*Shared Labs	*Labs in each Classroom
Fine Arts Spaces	*Shared practice rooms for music, choir, etc. *Art studio is off campus at community center	*Separate practice rooms for music, choir, etc *Art studio on campus
Teacher Offices	*Shared offices.	Separate offices
Cafeteria/Recreation Space	*1 cafeteria	*2 cafeterias *Student lounge with pool table.
Computer Labs	*Whole school shares computer resources *Lab time is scarce *Computers are close together	*Each department has it's own lab space *Lab time is easier to schedule *Computers are spread out and have table-top space for writing.
Other academic resources	*Library space performs many functions (college resource center, language listening lab, area for group work)	*Separate rooms for college resource center, language listening lab, area for group work. *Large multi-purpose room that teachers can schedule as needed.

Figure 3: Details of small and large building options *continued*

EXTRACURRICULAR	Small: 12 acres	Large: 24 acres
Athletics	*1 gymnasium *1 shared competition track and field for football, soccer, etc. *1 shared use practice field *2 baseball diamonds *Pool, tennis courts, and field space available at community center 13-minute bus ride away from campus. *1 weight room	*2 gymnasiums *Separate competition field for football *Soccer and track share competition field *3 practice fields *4 baseball diamonds *Field house *Pool *6 tennis courts *2 weight rooms
Theatre and Music	*1 mixed use auditorium space for theatre, orchestra, etc. *Marching band shares single practice field with athletics	*1 mixed use auditorium *1 drama theatre *Marching band has exclusive use of 1 practice field.
Clubs	*Clubs (chess, environment, politics, yearbook, etc) must use classroom space before or after school.	*6 dedicated club rooms for extracurricular activities

Constraints

Essential Question: *What are your constraints and considerations for designing the new school?*

Overview

Many factors often affect a final decision on a complicated problem. Thinking in terms of constraints and considerations can help you make sense of a difficult decision. Constraints are the limitations you are working under. They may be physical limitations or limitations that come from your personal values. For example, if there are only limited resources available, that is a physical constraint. If you refuse to destroy the habitat of a population of animals, that is a values-based constraint. Other constraints might include time, money, or laws.

Constraints are absolute limitations. They cannot be violated when coming up with a solution. Considerations are preferences that might or might not be possible. Decision makers keep in mind their constraints as they consider all available options. They also try to achieve as many important considerations as they can.

Procedure

Determine your personal constraints and considerations. Write out a list of each.

Analysis Questions

1. What would you consider a successful outcome?
2. What personal values will effect what you put on your considerations list?
3. Answer the essential question: What are your constraints and considerations for designing the new school?

Group Constraints and Considerations

Essential Question: *What made some considerations more important than others?*

Overview

When environmental decisions need to be made, there are often groups of people with very different ideas and solutions. The decisions you have made so far have been personal ones. In this project, you will need to work with your group to make a decision you can all agree on. You each have your own lists of constraints and considerations. Some parts of your lists will be the same and some will be different. Your task is to agree on a list that will guide your group through the rest of the project. This may be difficult, but it is important to agree now on your goals. The Environmental Decision Making Process will continue to appear in later lessons.

Materials

For each group:

- lists of personal constraints and considerations from each group member
- letter from Lesson 1*: Letter*

Procedure

As a group, you must come to an agreement on the constraints and considerations you will use to make your decision. Remember: Constraints are limits or rules you must not violate. Considerations are goals that you would like to achieve, but are not absolutely necessary.

Analysis Questions

1. What are the absolute constraints that your group agrees should not be violated in this situation?
2. What are the considerations that you would all like to achieve in this situation?
3. Rank your considerations from most important to least important.
4. Answer the essential question by justifying your ranking. Write at least two paragraphs. *What made some considerations more important than others?*

Lesson 2
Narrow Options

***Driving Question:** What are the consequences of building a school on this land?*

Overview

In this lesson, you will narrow your options to the three best ones. You will use your list of constraints and considerations as a guide. You will again work part of the time by yourself and part of the time with your group. Your task is to take the architect's building plans and find an appropriate place for each part of the school campus. You may have to build over important pieces of the ecosystem, possibly even gopher tortoise burrows. To explore the consequences of these actions, you will use Cascading Consequence Charts. Once the consequences are clear, you will move on to the next lesson on stakeholders.

Important Content

- Energy, water and land (especially arable land) are limited resources on Earth.
- Natural systems are complex and interdependent. Even land that may seem vacant is often alive with animal habitats, plant communities, and thriving ecosystems.
- Energy is transferred between animals and plants through trophic levels. All energy for living systems comes from the Sun.
- Animals and plants are interconnected in ecosystems in ways other than energy transfer. These relationships can be beneficial or harmful to the organisms involved. Non-living parts of the ecosystem (like fire) can also be part of these relationships.
- Disturbances to ecosystems (including loss of a species, disease, and pollution) can be man-made or natural. They can cause small problems or a catastrophic demise of a system.

Eliminate Options

Essential Question: *What school options violate your basic constraints?*

Overview

Now that you have your list of constraints and considerations, you need to consider the options available to you. To make this decision, you need to recall the Ecosystems chapter where you learned about the needs of the gopher tortoise. If you re-read Chapter 4, Lesson 1: *Gopher Tortoises* you will see that gopher tortoises need two land areas to survive. They need an area for burrowing and a range area where they search for food. All gopher tortoises need access to both of these areas. The tortoises usually build their burrows in the scrub plant community. Their range area can be in any community in the ecosystem – scrub, sandhill, scrubby flatwoods, or pine flatwoods. Many gopher tortoises live in groups, so there can be some overlap in their ranges. This is not a problem as long as there is not more than one tortoise per acre.

Analysis Questions

1. The requirement for a viable population of tortoises is 50. So how much land needs to be set aside for use only by the tortoises?

2. Fill out the chart on the next page to see which combinations of school buildings will allow for 50 tortoises to survive. The first example is filled out for you.

Academic Size	Parking Size	Extracurricular Size	Total used by school	Total for tortoises	Is it enough?	Does it meet your other constraints?
8 acres	4 acres	12 acres	24 acres	76 acres	YES	

3. Look at the map. Notice that part of the land is covered by the river. Is that land useful to the tortoise for foraging? Adjust your "Is it enough?" column to account for the land that the river covers.

4. In the last column of the chart, indicate whether the option listed meets your other constraints. Fill in the column with YES, NO, or MAYBE (if you need to do more research to see if the constraint is met).

   (For example, suppose one of your constraints is that the school must have a large parking lot. Then the example above does not meet your constraints and it would be marked NO.)

   (In the following activities, you will explore the options from the chart that have YES or MAYBE in both of the last two columns. If there is a NO in one of the columns, you don't need to explore that option.)

5. Answer the essential question: *What school options violate your basic constraints?*

Narrowing, Round 1

Essential Question: *How do these three choices fit the constraints and considerations YOU feel are most important?*

Overview

Look at the chart you created with your teammates in Lesson 2: *Eliminate Options*. Use the map of the school site and the pieces that represent the school buildings to explore your options. Try to find your three best options for size and placement of the school.

Materials

For each group:

- map and building pieces
- readings and food webs from *Ecosystems* chapter.

Safety

Use caution with sharp scissors; return all materials as instructed by your teacher.

Procedure

1. Cut out the school building pieces. Use them, along with the site map, to look at your options for the design of the school.

2. Your school design must include one academic building, one parking lot, and one extracurricular area.

3. Try out as many options as possible until you settle on three options that seem to be the best ones. Make notes or sketches to help you remember which buildings you used and where they were placed.

Analysis Questions

1. For your three best options, make Cascading Consequence Charts. Make sure your chart answers the following questions:

    a. What plant communities are being covered by school buildings? What effect will that have on the food web?

    b. How much area remains for the gopher tortoises? Can the tortoises get to the entire area easily? (Remember: gopher tortoises don't swim.)

    c. What effects will the placement of buildings have on the students?

2. Answer the essential question: *How do these three choices fit the constraints and considerations YOU feel are most important?*

Narrowing, Round 2

Essential Question: *What makes these three options the best?*

Overview

In this activity, you will compare the options you developed in Lesson 2: *Narrowing, Round 1.* As a group, you will need to reach a consensus about which three options are the best. (The three options that you choose should be very different from each other.) As you discuss the different options, remember to use evidence to support your position. Use the readings from Chapter 4: Ecosystems to better understand the consequences of altering the environment. Use your group's list of constraints and considerations to guide your choices and eliminate unsuitable options.

Materials

For each group:

- 3 options and consequence charts from each member of the group
- map and architectural cut-outs

Procedure

Discuss with your group the options that were developed. Select the best three possibilities. Use the consequence charts to help make your decision. Make sure that your options meet your constraints and considerations.

Remember to consider that:

- Gopher tortoises will not swim across the river. If you want the tortoises to be able to use the land across the river, you must provide them with access to that area. (Re-read Chapter 4, Lesson 1: *Gopher Tortoises* for hints.) If you do this, consider the consequences if your plan does not work and the animals do not have access to that land.
- All of the tortoises need access to each other. They also need access to appropriate burrowing and feeding areas. If your buildings block access to a needed area of the land, you need to consider the consequences.
- Covering most or all of one plant community could have serious effects on the food web. Review the readings and food web from the Ecosystems chapter to understand the impacts of eliminating certain plants or animals.

Analysis Questions

1. For each of the three options, your group should turn in:

   a. a sketch or complete description of the buildings you chose and the placement on the map.

   b. a Search Cascading Consequence chart with consequences to the environment, the school community and the gopher tortoises.

   c. a modified food web that shows which plants or animals will be reduced in numbers or destroyed.

   Remember: The three options you choose must be very different from each other!

2. Answer the essential question: *What makes these three options the best?*

Lesson 3
Evaluate and Compare

Driving Question: *Which of these options has the smallest number of unintended consequences?*

Overview

Use the consequence charts and food webs from the last lesson to explore your school placement choice. With your team, identify your stakeholders. Determine how important they are to your decision. Use the Stakeholders Chart from the Environmental Decision Making Process to organize this information. This chart will show you how stakeholders will be affected by your actions. In the next lesson, you will make your decision and present it to your classmates.

Important Content

- Energy, water and land (especially arable land) are limited resources on Earth.
- Natural systems are complex and interdependent. Even land that may seem vacant is often alive with animal habitats, plant communities, and thriving ecosystems.
- Energy is transferred between animals and plants through trophic levels. All energy for living systems comes from the Sun.
- Animals and plants are interconnected in ecosystems in ways other than energy transfer. These relationships can be beneficial or harmful to the organisms involved. Non-living parts of the ecosystem (like fire) can also be part of these relationships.
- Disturbances to ecosystems (including loss of a species, disease, and pollution) can be man-made or natural. They can cause small problems or a catastrophic demise of a system.

Investigate Impacts

Essential Questions: *Which stakeholders will be most affected by your decision? Are those stakeholders the ones who have the power to make the decision?*

Overview

You now have consequence charts and modified food webs for your three options. It is time to look more closely at your options. In this activity, you will construct stakeholder charts for the options that you chose in the last lesson. Remember that stakeholders are people, organizations, the environment, etc., that will be affected by your decision. The chart you make in this activity will help you organize the consequences in a different way. You will see all the ways that each stakeholder will be affected. It is important to note whether the effect is your intended goal or a side effect. Decisions having many unintended side effects might not be the best to make. One aspect of side effects, and negative effects in general, is consent. Did the stakeholder consent to be a part of this process or decision? Think about the responsibilities that decision makers have for the consequences of their actions.

Procedure

1. Based on your consequence charts and food webs, create a list of stakeholders.
2. As a group, complete the first five columns of the stakeholders chart for each of the options.

Analysis Questions

1. How did you narrow your list of stakeholders?
2. How are the stakeholders related to your list of constraints and criteria?
3. Do you believe that decision makers are responsible for the unintended effects of the decisions that they make? Why or why not?
4. Answer the essential questions: Which stakeholders will be most affected by your decision? Are those stakeholders the ones who have the power to make the decision?

Stakeholders for Option #1

Who are the stakeholders that will be affected by this action?	In what way(s) will they be affected?	+ or –	Is this effect the intended goal of the action or is it a side effect?	Has the stakeholder placed themselves in this position voluntarily and with an understanding of the risks involved?	How important to *you* are the interests of this stakeholder? 1=very important 2= somewhat important 3=unimportant	If the effect is negative, do *you* feel it is directly offset by greater good elsewhere?

Stakeholders for Option #2

Who are the stakeholders that will be affected by this action?	In what way(s) will they be affected?	+ or –	Is this effect the intended goal of the action or is it a side effect?	Has the stakeholder placed themselves in this position voluntarily and with an understanding of the risks involved?	How important to *you* are the interests of this stakeholder? 1=very important 2= somewhat important 3=unimportant	If the effect is negative, do *you* feel it is directly offset by greater good elsewhere?

Stakeholders for Option #3

Who are the stakeholders that will be affected by this action?	In what way(s) will they be affected?	+ or –	Is this effect the intended goal of the action or is it a side effect?	Has the stakeholder placed themselves in this position voluntarily and with an understanding of the risks involved?	How important to *you* are the interests of this stakeholder? 1=very important 2= somewhat important 3=unimportant	If the effect is negative, do *you* feel it is directly offset by greater good elsewhere?

Evaluate Impacts

Essential Question: *What personal values held by everyone in the group have affected the way the group ranked each stakeholder?*

Overview

Use your list of stakeholders. With a full understanding of the effects of your decision, think about the importance of each stakeholder.

Procedure

Finish the last two columns of the stakeholder worksheet with your group.

Analysis Questions

1. Do you agree with the group's decision in the ranking of stakeholders?
2. In what way is your ranking related to your constraints and considerations?
3. Do you want to change your constraints and considerations to reflect what you have learned during this process? Why or why not?
4. Answer the essential question: *What personal values held by everyone in the group have affected the way the group ranked each stakeholder?*

Lesson 4
Decide and Present

Driving Questions: *Which aspects of the decision were most important for your group? How will you communicate your decision to your classmates?*

Overview

You have reached the moment of truth! All of your information is gathered. You know the consequences of each option you researched. You just need to make the choice and justify it with an explanation. In this lesson, you will work with your group to select the best option and explain your decision to your classmates. You should use all of the information you have collected in this unit to support your explanation. Utilize your knowledge of constraints and considerations, ecosystems and gopher tortoise food webs, and population growth and the resources that populations consume. Your final argument will demonstrate that you understand the effects of growing populations on the Earth's land resources.

Important Content

- Energy, water and land (especially arable land) are limited resources on Earth.
- Natural systems are complex and interdependent. Even land that may seem vacant is often alive with animal habitats, plant communities, and thriving ecosystems.
- Energy is transferred between animals and plants through trophic levels. All energy for living systems comes from the Sun.
- Animals and plants are interconnected in ecosystems in ways other than energy transfer. These relationships can be beneficial or harmful to the organisms involved. Non-living parts of the ecosystem (like fire) can also be part of these relationships.
- Disturbances to ecosystems (including loss of a species, disease, and pollution) can be man-made or natural. They can cause small problems or a catastrophic demise of a system.

Make a Decision

Essential Question: *What is the best decision? Take into account all stakeholders, consequences, constraints, and considerations?*

Analysis Question

1. Answer the essential question: *What is the best decision? Take into account all stakeholders, consequences, constraints, and considerations?*

   Address each constraint and consideration that you listed.

   Explain why any negative effects are outweighed by the positive effects.

Present Your Decision

Essential Question: *What were the major obstacles to this decision?*

Overview

An important part of environmental decision making is supporting your claims with evidence. Assemble your report and prepare your presentation. Remember that you are trying to convince people that your decision is a good one. Use evidence from Ecosystems to support Chapter 4: your ideas. Describe logically why you made the decisions you did. Give reasons why you rejected some options. It is important to include your values and opinions in explaining your decision. Make sure that what you are saying is backed up with facts and evidence.

Procedure

1. Compile a report that includes:
   - a list of your group constraints and considerations.
   - a complete description of the three best options.
   - food webs, consequence charts, and stakeholder charts for all three options.
   - a decision statement that describes how you met each constraint and consideration.

2. Answer the analysis questions listed below.

3. Give a 5-minute presentation that includes:
   - a map of your chosen option.
   - a summary of why you chose the option you did.
   - evidence and information from the ecosystems chapter to describe how you re-drew your food web.

Analysis Questions

1. Are you satisfied with your decision? Why or why not?

2. Is there anything you would change if you had the chance to make the decision again?

3. What new information might lead you to rethink the decision you made?

4. Answer the essential question: *What were the major obstacles to this decision?*

Glossary

Abiotic – the physical and chemical aspects of an organism's environment

Age group – a group of people whose ages are approximately the same or fall within a stated range

Allochthonous – used to describe flora, fauna, or inhabitants that have moved to the region in which they are found from elsewhere

Amensalism – an interaction between populations of two species that harms one but not the other

Armadillo – a burrowing mammal with a hard-plated body, found in temperate and tropical regions of the Americas

Autotrophs – organisms that are capable of capturing sunlight and converting it to forms that can be used to synthesize organic compounds from inorganic materials

Bioaccumulation – build-up of toxins in the bodies of organisms within the food chain

Biological productivity – refers to nature's ability to reproduce and regenerate living matter. Biological productivity of a given land category (i.e., pasture, forest, etc.) is determined by dividing the total biological production (how much is grown and living on the land) by the total land area available in this category.

Biomagnification – the increasing concentration of toxins as they move up the food chain

Biotic – the features of a natural system that are living

Birth rate – the number of live births per 1,000 members of the population in a year

Blackout – a failure of an electrical supply

Burrow – a hole or tunnel dug as a living space by a small animal

Carnivore – an animal that eats other animals

Carrying capacity – the size of a population a region can support in terms of its resources

Climate – the average weather or the regular variations in weather in a region over a period of years

Closed system – a combination of related elements organized into a complex whole that is self-sustaining and self-regulating, without influence or interaction with outside elements

Commensal – a relationship between organisms of two different species in which one derives food or other benefits from the association while the other remains unharmed and unaffected

Community – all the plants and animals that live in the same area and interact with one another

Consequence – something that follows as a result

Consideration – something to be taken into account when considering the pros and cons before making a decision

Consumable goods – articles for sale or use (as opposed to services) that are bought by consumers and are not used to produce other goods

Control variables – aspects of the experimental setup that are held constant across trials

Criteria – an accepted standard used in making decisions or judgments about something

Culture – biological material, especially plants, microorganisms, or animal tissue, grown in a nutrient substance culture medium in specially controlled conditions for scientific, medical, or commercial purposes

Daphnia – a tiny freshwater crustacean with a transparent shell and branched antennae for swimming

Death rate – the number of deaths per 1,000 members of the population in a year

Decomposer – an organism, especially a bacterium or fungus, that causes organic matter to rot or decay

Dependent variable – outcomes of an experimental setup that are measured by the experimenter – for example, the size of the Daphnia population

Detrivores – organisms, such as bacteria and fungi that feed on dead remains of other organisms

Diatom – a microscopic one-celled alga that has silica-filled cell walls or shells divided into two halves

Dipper – a small plain-colored bird that lives beside rivers and can swim and dive

Ecological deficit – the situation that occurs when human demand exceeds ecological production and there are not enough resources to support the current human population in a way that maintains possible production for future generations

Ecological footprint – the land and water area that is required to support a defined human population and material standard indefinitely, using prevailing technology

Ecologically productive land – land that is fertile enough to support forests, agriculture and/or animal life

Ecotone – a zone of transition between two different ecosystems

Efficient – able to function well or achieve a desired result without waste

Emigration – the act of people leaving a country or specified area

Essential amino acids – amino acids the body cannot produce and therefore are obtained from an individual's diet

Exponential growth – rapidly becoming greater in size

Fertility – the ability to produce offspring

Food chain – a hierarchy of different living things, each of which feeds on the one below

Food web – the interlocking food chains within an ecological community

Geographic information – data that is linked to a geographic location

Glacier – a large body of continuously accumulating ice and compacted snow, formed in mountain valleys or at the poles, that deforms under its own weight and slowly moves

Ground water – water held underground in soil or permeable rock, often feeding springs and wells

Habitat – the natural conditions and environment in which a plant or animal lives

Herbivore – an animal that feeds only on plants

Herbivorous – eating only or mainly grass or other plants

Heterotrophs – organisms that obtain carbon and metabolic energy from organic molecules that have already been assembled by autotrophs

Histogram – a statistical graph of a frequency distribution in which vertical rectangles of different heights are proportionate to corresponding frequencies

Host – a human, animal, plant, or other organism in or on which another organism, especially a parasite, lives

Ice cap – a thick permanent covering of ice and snow extending outward in every direction; for example, from the North and South Poles or from a mountain top

Immigration – the act of people entering into a new country or area to settle permanently

Independent variables – aspects of an experimental setup that are changed by the experimenter such that they vary across trials

Interdependence – reliance on mutual assistance, support, cooperation, or interaction among constituent elements or members

Keystone species – an organism that supports and maintains the well-being of several other species

Kilowatt hour – a unit of energy equal to the work done by one kilowatt in one hour

Kingfisher – a brightly colored bird that usually has a short tail, a long stout bill, and sometimes a crest. It feeds on fish, insects, and other prey.

Latitude – an imaginary line joining points on the Earth's surface that are all of equal distance north or south of the equator

Leafhopper – a slender, spindle-shaped, leaping insect found worldwide that sucks the sap from plants and spreads plant diseases

Legend – an explanation of the symbols used on a map

Longitude – the angular distance east or west of the prime meridian that stretches from the North Pole to the South Pole and passes through Greenwich, England

Macrophyte – a plant large enough to be studied and observed using the unaided eye, especially an aquatic plant

Mercury – a poisonous, heavy, silver-white, metallic chemical element that is liquid at room temperature

Midge – a small, slender, flying insect that lives globally, particularly in swarms near bodies of standing water

Migration – the act or process of moving from one region or country to another

Mutualistic (mutualism/symbiosis) – a relationship between two organisms of different species that benefits both and harms neither

Neutralism – a situation where there is no relationship between populations of different species in an ecosystem

Niche – the role of an organism within its natural environment that determines its relations with other organisms and ensures its survival

Non-essential amino acids – amino acids the body can produce

Omnivore – an animal that will feed on both plants and animals

Parasitic – living in or on another host organism, usually causing it harm without killing it

Parasitism – organisms that take their nourishment by living either inside or outside another organism, causing it harm without killing it

Predator – a carnivorous animal that hunts, kills, and eats other animals in order to survive, or any other organism that behaves in a similar manner

Prey – an animal or animals that are caught, killed, and eaten by another animal

Primary consumer – an eater of primary producers

Primary producer – a producer of food, like an autotroph

Protein – a complex organic compound made up of chains of smaller chemicals called amino acids

Protozoan – a single-celled organism such as an amoeba that can move and feeds on organic compounds of nitrogen and carbon

Query – finding an answer to a question in ArcView based on the data in themes

Reproduction – the production of young plants and animals of the same kind through a sexual or asexual process

Rural – sparsely populated, mostly farmland or natural vegetation such as forest

Salinization – to treat or contaminate something with salt

Saw PawPaw – a small North American deciduous tree or shrub of the custard apple family that has large oblong leaves, purple or white flowers, and small fleshy edible fruit

Sculpin – a marine and freshwater fish, mostly bottom-dwelling, with a large flat head, large pectoral fins, and spines

Secondary consumer – an eater of primary consumers

Solar energy – using the Sun's radiation as a source of energy

Soluble – able to be dissolved in another substance

Suburban – used to describe an area not as populated as cities, usually located near a major city

Succession – the series of changes that create a full-fledged plant and animal community; for example, from the colonization of bare rock to the establishment of a forest

Sustainability – the ability of a system to continue and maintain a production level or quality of life for future generations

Tertiary consumer – an eater of secondary consumers

Toxin – any substance said to accumulate in the body that is considered to be harmful or poisonous to the system

Trade-off – a situation in which somebody is prepared to compromise by giving up all or part of one thing in exchange for another

Trophic Level – the number of steps away from an autotroph that the animal is on a food chain

Turbellarian – a free-living flatworm such as a planarian that inhabits wet soil, freshwater, and marine environments

Urban – used to describe densely populated cities

Vacant – having no occupant or contents

Vole – a small rodent mammal

Waterlogging – becoming saturated with water

Index